"What can you do? Cook for your community and yourself. Simple food—honestly sourced and lovingly made—creates connections, gives fuel to the fight, starves ignorance and apathy. Where to start? With a spoon and a pot and this inspiring, instructive book."

—ADAM SACHS, Editor in Chief, *Saveur*

"Julia Turshen is my 'shero.' In *Feed the Resistance,* she gives us a manifesto for food activism. From essays by fellow food fighters like Bryant Terry, Caleb Zigas, and Shakirah Simley to a resource list for novices to recipes that can feed small gatherings or multitudes, she blazes a trail for those who want to use food to create change. If that weren't enough, all profits go to the ACLU. Buy this book and begin your own food journey."

—DR. JESSICA B. HARRIS, Culinary Historian and Author, *My Soul Looks Back*

FEED THE RESISTANCE

FEED

THE

RESISTANCE

RECIPES + IDEAS FOR GETTING INVOLVED

JULIA TURSHEN

WITH CONTRIBUTIONS FROM

JOCELYN DELK ADAMS, MAYA-CAMILLE
BROUSSARD, ANTHONY THOSH COLLINS AND
CHELSEY LUGER, ERIKA COUNCIL, DEVITA
DAVISON, CHERYL DAY, VON DIAZ, YANA
GILBUENA, MIKKI HALPIN, HAWA HASSAN,
JOCELYN JACKSON, CALLIE JAYNE, JORDYN
LEXTON, PREETI MISTRY, PEOPLE'S KITCHEN
COLLECTIVE, STEPHEN SATTERFIELD, NIK
SHARMA, SHAKIRAH SIMLEY, BILL SMITH
AND ANTONIO LOPEZ, BRYANT TERRY, TUNDE
WEY, AND CALEB ZIGAS

CHRONICLE BOOKS
SAN FRANCISCO

For Jennie, because it takes a village
and I'm so grateful that you are mine.

Library of Congress Cataloging-in-Publication Data .
Names: Turshen, Julia, author.
Title: Feed the resistance : practical and purposeful recipes + ideas for
   getting involved / Julia Turshen with contributions from Maya-Camille
   Broussard, Anthony Thosh Collins and Chelsea Luger, Erika Council, Devita
   Davison, Cheryl Day, Jocelyn Delk Adams, Von Diaz, Yana Gilbuena, Mikki
   Halpin, Hawa Hassan, Jocelyn Jackson, Callie Jayne, Jordyn Lexton, Preeti
   Mistry, People's Kitchen Collective, Stephen Satterfield, Nik Sharma,
   Shakirah Simley, Bill Smith and Antonio Lopez, Bryant Terry, Tunde Wey,
   and Caleb Zigas.
Description: San Francisco : Chronicle Books, [2017] | Includes index.
Identifiers: LCCN 2017024414 | ISBN 9781452168388 (hc : alk. paper)
Subjects: LCSH: Cooking. | LCGFT: Cookbooks.
Classification: LCC TX714 .T878 2017 | DDC 641.5—dc23 LC record available at
https://lccn.loc.gov/2017024414

Manufactured in the United States of America.
Design by **Vanessa Dina**
Typestting by **Frank Brayton**

10 9 8 7 6 5 4 3 2 1

Chronicle books and gifts are available at special quantity discounts to corporations,
professional associations, literacy programs, and other organizations. For details and discount
information, please contact our premiums department at corporatesales@chroniclebooks
.com or at 1-800-759-0190.

Chronicle Books LLC
680 Second Street
San Francisco, California 94107
www.chroniclebooks.com

FEEDING THE MASSES: FOOD FOR CROWDS 52

BAKED GOODS + PORTABLE SNACKS 106

INTRO-
DUCTION

Seven days into Donald J. Trump's presidency, six days after so many of us marched across the world, I sat in a church recreation room with my wife, Grace, near our home in the Hudson Valley at an immigrants' rights meeting. We were listening to a local organizer explain in two languages how to know and protect your rights and how to be an active ally. As we listened, news alerts went off on phones, *ding ding* all over the room, giving us all updates on the first version of the travel ban the President wished to enforce. It felt as if no matter how quickly we rallied to find a solution, the problem itself wouldn't even stand still. Change, it's been said, is the only constant. In that moment we were reminded so clearly that resistance must always be change's companion. Complacency was no longer a privilege any of us could continue to afford.

In this new world, which in so many ways isn't new at all and is just old without the guise of false security, resistance is the new normal. Many have been getting into what Georgia Congressman John Lewis refers to as "good trouble" for decades. For some, activism is inherited and tightly woven into their fabric. For others, activism is a less ingrained part of life, a match just struck.

We're living in a time of upheaval and the call to activism is loud and clear. In figuring out the shape of my own activism, I keep thinking about heroes, about folks like John Lewis who don't wait for permission or instruction. I am constantly reminded that heroes operate in all different ways. Many are loud, while many embody that beautiful Rumi quotation to "Raise your words, not voice. It is rain that grows flowers, not thunder."

I am fairly new to regular activism. While I am a gay, Jewish woman living in rural America, at the end of the day I am a white, able-bodied, cisgender, educated, financially secure person in America. Therefore my resistance has always been on my own terms. I have always had the luxury of choosing when, where, and how I want to be active in my community (if at all). I understand how rare this is.

A silver lining of this new administration is the transformation of so many folks, myself included, from being sometimes activists to being fully committed members of the resistance. It's no longer a few sprints here and there. It's a marathon and our cadence is ours to determine, so long as we keep moving.

For me, that movement comes in the form of feeding people in all the ways I know how, but doing so with greater purpose and recruiting others to do the same since we are indeed stronger and more capable together. I have always regularly volunteered with food pantries, hunger relief organizations, and programs like God's Love We Deliver and Angel Food East (they both provide homemade meals for people homebound with chronic illness). But I haven't always quite seen the connection between this kind of work part and the resistance. It took something else for me to connect the dots.

A few days after the meeting in the church, Grace and I were on our way out of another meeting in our community at Citizen Action of New York, a statewide group with a local branch not too far from our home. "Did I hear you say you knew about food?" Callie, the meeting leader, asked me as I reached for the door. I told her I did and that I write cookbooks. "So you're organized. You can be our Food Team Leader." When I asked her what the Food Team was, she informed me that it wasn't yet. That I would be starting it. In that moment, Callie let me know exactly how I could both reframe the work I was already doing and also amplify it. I know food and I know how to effectively organize. Why not just put those skills toward feeding, quite literally, the resistance?

From that day forward I was put in charge of communicating with other folks in our community who also love to cook and wanted to do something helpful. Together we would make sure there was something to eat at every single meeting at our Citizen Action branch. Together we would make sure folks like Callie and other organizers didn't have to think about what was for dinner. In saving them that time and providing the food, they could continue their important work and be guaranteed the comfort and nourishment of a homemade meal. Just like cooking for people in my community who cannot cook for themselves, feeding the resistance was something I could, and continue to, happily commit to. An extension of my profession and my passion, this work fuels me, too. Finding that connection makes the work, and my resistance, sustainable.

In this work I am constantly reminded that food has true power. On the most basic level, resistance, just like any other active thing, needs to be fed in order to sustain. Beyond that, food touches on just about every single issue that matters. Being interested in food, really caring about it, has a domino effect. You start caring about where it comes from, what it means to the people you are feeding, and what it means to be fed.

To think deeply about food is to also think deeply about the environment, the economy, immigration, education, community, culture, families, race, gender, and identity. Food is about people, all people. It is the most democratic thing in the world, lower-case "d," and affects all of us. All of us. It is the thing we, the entire world!, all have in common. Therefore it also has the power to inform us about where we come from, inform how we express and share ourselves, and ultimately has the power to bring us together with empathetic understanding. It is no wonder that bread, fruit, wine, and even water itself are symbols in just about every religion and culture.

Food is also so wonderfully tangible. Part of why I love to cook is because there's such a clear sense of completion and accomplishment. In all times, but especially during uncertain ones, there is something so beautifully comforting about cooking a meal from start to finish. Peeling and slicing onions and watching them soften in hot butter might not be the answer to world peace, but it is nice to know that when I do just that, I am one of millions around the world doing that exact thing at the exact same time. When we cook, we are in solidarity. There is power in that.

Cooking cannot only balm our emotions and sustain, it is also a constant reminder of transformation and possibility. Just watch things like flour and buttermilk get stirred together into a shaggy dough and then, just like that, stand tall in the oven as they become bronzed biscuits. Cooking shows us over and over again that we can make things happen, we can make change happen, with just our own hands. Food is metaphor personified and within that there is reaffirmation of what we can accomplish.

This book happened really quickly. I realized that the work I was doing in my own community could be exponential if I put some of it down on paper and shared it with you so that you can better feed your own resistance, whatever that looks like, and hopefully share it with those around you.

Feed the Resistance is a mix of practical and purposeful and it features contributions from some of the smartest and most inspiring people I know. Putting this book together offered me the chance to reflect a lot on not just what I cook in my kitchen, but what others cook in theirs and what food means to all of us. There are three categories of recipes here.

The first, Easy Meals for Folks Who Are Too Busy Resisting to Cook, is full of simple recipes for quick, healthy meals (these truly double for anyone busy, so that means you families, multitaskers, working parents, and students!). There's everything from a Thai Yellow Curry Vegetable Pot (page 48) to my friend Von Diaz's Arroz a Caballo (page 24) and Nik Sharma's Spiced Mung Bean Wraps (page 22).

The second category, Feeding the Masses: Food for Crowds, includes the most incredible range of recipes all geared toward groups. From Bryant Terry's totally vegan

Dark Roux Mushroom Gumbo (page 54) to Devita Davison's family recipe for Southern-Style Boiled Cabbage with Smoked Turkey (page 74) and Preeti Mistry's incredibly delicious Tikka Masala Macaroni + Cheese (page 98), these recipes are all about getting a large amount of food on a table with lots of intention but without spending a fortune on ingredients or time.

The third and final category, Baked Goods + Portable Snacks, features some of the most meaningful recipes. There are biscuits from Erika Council (page 108), the same ones she watched her grandmother make on Sundays to feed children without enough to eat. There's Jocelyn Delk Adams's Spiced Brown Sugar Pound Cake with Rum Molasses Glaze (page 117), the cake she says to make "when your soul needs food in the midst of the fight." There are Chocolate Espresso Pie Bars (page 119) from the lovely Cheryl Day inspired by Georgia Gilmore's "The Club From Nowhere," a group of women who sold homemade baked goods to offset transportation funds during the bus boycotts in Montgomery, Alabama, during the 1950s. Those women remind us that even if you don't have a formal group in your area, you can still feed the resistance in purposeful ways.

Cheryl's recipe is also a good reminder that while this book happened quickly, its roots are way older than this administration, and, needless to say, myself. The contents of this book stand on the shoulders of other moments in time when resisting was a way of being and required understanding, compassion, action, and nourishing food to be sustainable. As the saying goes, there's nothing new under the sun . . . especially when it comes to both food and politics.

Thinking about food in this holistic sense brings us to the essays placed throughout the book. *Feed the Resistance* has more than just recipes for things to cook. It also has recipes for understanding and fueling activism. Callie gives us her ground rules to help us approach activism, just like Mikki Halpin's "Practical Activism: If You Want to Do Something, Don't Try to Do Everything" helps us navigate it. Shakirah Simley so evocatively reflects on race and identity in her essay and shows how these reflections have helped inspire her own activism. Jordyn Lexton and Caleb Zigas both beautifully explain how food is at the core of their work and the power it has to transform lives and communities.

The book closes with lists of resources and concrete ideas for ways to engage and get involved. Oh, and as I hope it's clear from the cover, all proceeds from this book go directly to the American Civil Liberties Union. So by purchasing it, you've already begun to support the resistance. How about that?

I hope you get as much out of reading this book as I got out of putting it together. Working on this book has taught me more than ever that food's power is mirrored only by our own.

In solidarity and community and with love,

JULIA TURSHEN
Spring 2017

PRACTICAL ACTIVISM: IF YOU WANT TO DO SOMETHING, DON'T TRY TO DO EVERYTHING

By Mikki Halpin, Author of *It's Your World: If You Don't Like It, Change It,* Creator of tinyletter.com/actionnow

Sometimes I feel like there is too much activism out there. I see so many people who feel like they need to go to every protest, attend every meeting, send every e-mail, sign every petition, and make every phone call. These people are usually exhausted. To be perfectly honest, these people are not making that much of a difference.

I want to tell them: Don't do everything. Don't even try to do everything. You won't. You can't. You seriously can't. Trying to do everything will not only burn you out, it's not effective. If you want to act on your values and help make this a better world, put your energy where it will have the most impact. If you want to be an activist, be a practical one.

Being a practical activist means getting real about what you can and can't do. It's not easy but you will have to let some things go. It doesn't mean that you don't care about those things—it means that you are opting for engagement over visibility. It means you are going to prioritize working over talking. It means that you are ready to really commit to showing up for what you believe in.

Being a practical activist means being a community activist. The issues that you are about aren't abstract—they are all around you. Not only that, there are people all around you who care about them, too. Finding that community and acting together on your shared values is a powerful tool for change. You can do it! Here's how:

Think about the causes you are passionate about and choose three:

One you'll be a leader on
One you'll be a follower on
One you'll make a habit of

Then use this framework to organize how you spend your time and energy.

In the area where you've chosen to be a leader, you'll be setting goals and inspiring others to action. (You might also be part of a leadership team.) How can your community make progress on the issue you've chosen to work on? If you care about reproductive rights, maybe you'll start a group that holds a fundraiser for a different independent abortion clinic every month. If you're worried about climate change, you might decide to pressure your city to divest from Dakota Access Pipeline (DAPL) and other dangerous pipelines—or you could work to get more trees planted in neighborhoods that need them. If you care about mental health, maybe you'll start an online initiative to get more volunteers for the Crisis Text Line.

Being a practical leader means not reinventing the wheel—don't start something that already exists. It means respecting those with more experience than you have. It means making sure everyone is heard at meetings, especially people of color, women, members of the LGBTQ community, and people with disabilities—and it means recognizing that all those things intersect. It means that people with privilege, including yourself, should focus on listening. It means creating a space where people can be wrong, and people can fail, and the work can continue.

Where you've chosen to be a follower, you'll be an active participant, but taking on less responsibility than you would if you were a leader. You help, but you aren't in charge. In the abortion group example, you might be the person who finds the venue for every event. Or maybe you are the one who researches alternative banks that don't fund DAPL for your divestment project. You might join a group that's part of a national organization like Indivisible that already has a set agenda. Being a follower doesn't mean you're a slacker—it's active participation.

Being a practical follower means pitching in to do what needs to be done, whether it's stuffing envelopes or making phone calls or going door to door, even if you're a filmmaker in real life. It means you contribute ideas, you do outreach, you show up. It means realizing that not all activism is visible or Instagrammable. But even when you are a "follower," you're accountable for doing the things you said you would.

When it comes to choosing your activism "habit," look for a repeatable action organized by someone else that you can do routinely without a huge amount of effort. That could be doing a shift at a food pantry every week, or making the phone call suggested in every Planned Parenthood e-mail, or going to every event organized by your local immigrant rights group. It's something you are committed to, but you aren't spending a lot of mental energy on it.

Being a practical activist doesn't mean that you don't care about the issues you aren't working directly on. You can still support them in any way you want. But focusing your activism, and your energy, will allow you to make a greater and more sustainable commitment to the things you believe in. Activism is acting on your values— practical activism means being smart about it. We've got a lot of work to do.

(This essay is adapted from the newsletter sent on January 24, 2017.)

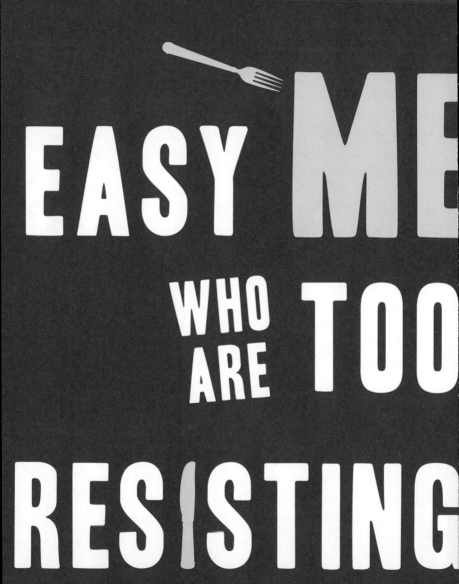

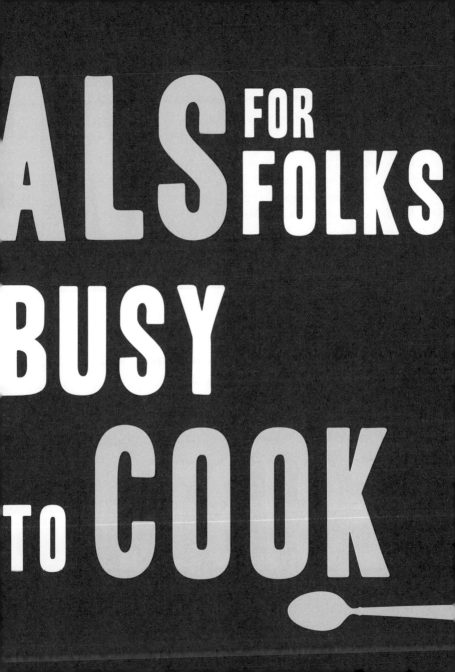

Spiced Mung Bean Wraps

Legumes and lentils are among the cheapest sources of nourishment and protein for most vegetarians, especially in countries such as India. Besides being rich in nutritious amino acids and proteins, they also contribute fiber. This simple yet flavorful filling is made up of sprouted mung beans, fresh herbs, and feta all encased in a whole-grain tortilla, making it easy to pack and travel with. You could also chop up and toss in four hardboiled eggs to bump up the protein.

MAKES 4 WRAPS

½ cup [80 g] sprouted mung beans (see Note)
¼ cup [60 ml] vegetable oil
1 medium white or yellow onion, diced
2 garlic cloves, minced
One 1-in [2.5-cm] piece peeled fresh ginger, finely grated
1 Tbsp red pepper flakes
1 tsp ground turmeric
1 Tbsp freshly squeezed lemon juice
1 Tbsp chopped fresh cilantro leaves
1 Tbsp chopped fresh mint leaves
½ cup [60 g] crumbled feta cheese
Kosher salt
Freshly ground black pepper
4 whole-grain tortillas

Rinse and drain the sprouted mung beans under cold running water and place them on a clean kitchen towel to dry.

Place the oil in a large skillet on medium-high heat. Add the onion and cook, stirring now and then, until translucent, 7 to 8 minutes. Add the garlic and ginger and cook, stirring constantly, until fragrant, about 30 seconds. Add the red pepper flakes and turmeric and cook for another 30 seconds. Decrease the heat to medium-low and fold in the rinsed mung beans. Cover the skillet and cook, uncovering it to give it a stir now and then, until the beans are softened but still retain a little bite, about 25 minutes. Turn off the heat and stir in the lemon juice, cilantro, mint, and feta. Season to taste with salt and pepper.

Divide the bean mixture among the four tortillas and wrap to form burritos. Serve immediately or hold for up to 6 hours.

NOTE: If you can't find sprouted mung beans (they're available at many farmers' markets), they're easy to make yourself. Start with ½ cup [80 g] dry mung beans and pick out any stones and dirt. Rinse them clean under cold running tap water and then place them in a bowl and cover with 1 in [2.5 cm] cold water. Cover the bowl and let the beans sit in a cool, dark place for 6 to 12 hours. Drain the beans, rinse, and place them on a large piece of wet cheesecloth (about 2 layers is good). Bring the ends of the cloth together, tie the beans up in a "bag," and then place the bag in a jar or large bowl and loosely cover with a kitchen towel. Place in a cool, dark place, rinsing the bag once a day until the beans sprout, 4 to 5 days. Rinse the sprouted beans with cold water before using. Keep the sprouted beans out of sunlight or else they get bitter.

Variations on Arroz a Caballo

When my mom was growing up in Puerto Rico, my grand-mother—whom I call Tata—picked her up from school at lunchtime every day so she could eat at home. Some-times they had leftovers, but often Tata would make arroz a caballo. Literally translated as "horse-style rice," it's essentially white rice served with a fried egg on top and ketchup. The origins of its name vary wildly, but it's among my family's favorite cheap quick meals.

But rice with meat or egg and seasoning is certainly not unique to Puerto Rico. Spanish paella, Korean bibim-bap, Nigerian jollof rice, and Chinese fried rice all bear a striking resemblance to the flavor profile of this humble, affordable, and quick comfort food.

Today, I often make arroz a caballo for myself using leftover stock, scraps of meat and vegetable, and whatever tasty condiments I have around. It's a great way to use up random ingredients you purchased for a recipe, or bits of meat and vegetables that aren't enough for a full meal. When making the classic version, I prefer basmati to the plain rice my family used. But here are three "fancified" versions using some of my favorite fridge and pantry sta-ples. Special thanks to Mario Schambon for helping design and test these recipes.

SERVES 4

Classic Arroz a Caballo

1 cup [175 g] Perfect Basmati Rice (page 29)
1 Perfect Fried Egg (page 28)
Salt and pepper for seasoning
1 tsp ketchup, or more, for seasoning

Mound the cooked rice in a soup bowl. Fry the egg, and immediately after frying scoop the egg onto the rice using a spatula. Season with salt, pepper, and ketchup to taste.

Arroz a Caballo with Greens and Smoked Pork

1 tsp ketchup
¼ tsp Sriracha or other hot sauce
1 Tbsp olive oil
1 Tbsp diced smoked pork (such as prosciutto, pancetta, bacon, or ham)
Generous handful chopped greens (such as spinach, kale, arugula, chard)
1 Perfect Fried Egg (fried in olive oil; page 28)
1 cup [175 g] Perfect Brown Rice (page 30)
1 Tbsp store-bought French-fried onions (the ones that typically go on green bean casserole, optional)
Salt and pepper for seasoning

Combine the ketchup and Sriracha in a small bowl, and mix well with a fork.

In a medium skillet, heat the olive oil over medium-high heat until simmering, about 30 seconds. Add the diced smoked pork and sauté for 1 minute, stirring continuously. Add the greens and sauté until just wilted; remove from the heat and set aside.

Meanwhile, fry the egg. Once the greens and egg are fully cooked, scoop the rice into a soup bowl. Top with the greens and pork and place the egg on top with a spatula. Sprinkle with the French-fried onions if you're using them. Season with the ketchup-Sriracha mixture and salt and pepper to taste.

Arroz a Caballo with Sardines and Capers

1 Tbsp ketchup
½ tsp chipotle sauce (optional)
1 Perfect Fried Egg (fried in olive oil; page 28)
1 cup [175 g] Perfect Basmati Rice (page 29)
1 canned sardine fillet, preferably smoked in tomato sauce
1 tsp capers, drained
Salt and pepper for seasoning

Combine the ketchup and chipotle sauce (if using) in a small bowl, and mix well with a fork.

Meanwhile, fry the egg. Once the egg is cooked, scoop the rice into a soup bowl. Top with the sardine fillet and capers and place the egg on top using a spatula. Season with salt, pepper, and the ketchup mixture to taste.

Arroz a Caballo with Miso Shiitake Butter and Kimchi

1½ cups [360 ml] water
1 tsp white miso paste
1 Tbsp plus ½ tsp unsalted butter
½ tsp dried shrimp (optional)
¾ cup [45 g] fresh shiitake mushrooms, thinly sliced or
   2 Tbsp dried, reconstituted in hot water
1 Perfect Fried Egg (fried in butter; page 28)
1 cup [175 g] Perfect Black Rice (page 29)
½ cup [130 g] baek-kimchi (white kimchi, store-bought)
1 Tbsp thinly sliced seasoned laver (dried seaweed)
Salt and pepper for seasoning
Hot sauce for seasoning

Prepare the miso butter by bringing the water to a boil in a small saucepan over medium-high heat. Add the miso paste and whisk to incorporate. Decrease the heat to medium and simmer until the mixture is reduced by half, 7 to 10 minutes. Add 1 Tbsp of the butter and swirl the pan continuously for 30 to 45 seconds, until the butter is fully incorporated. Add the dried shrimp (if using) and continue swirling the pan until fragrant, about 30 seconds. Add the mushrooms and cook 1 more minute, until tender. Add the remaining ½ tsp butter, swirl the pan to incorporate, then remove from the heat and cover until ready to use. The miso butter should be thick and creamy. Note: you need ½ cup miso butter for this recipe, but it makes 1 cup (you can store it covered in the fridge for a week).

Meanwhile, fry the egg. Once the miso butter and egg are fully cooked, scoop the cooked rice into a soup bowl. Top with ½ cup of the miso butter and place the egg on top with a spatula. Garnish with the white kimchi and seasoned laver, then season with salt, pepper, and hot sauce to taste.

A Perfect Fried Egg

MAKES 1 PERFECT EGG

2 Tbsp butter or olive oil
1 large egg

Heat the butter or olive oil in a 6-in [15-cm] nonstick skillet over medium-high heat until the butter is melted but not sizzling, about 30 seconds. Decrease the heat to low and crack the egg into the pan. Let the pan rest on the burner for a moment until the egg begins to cook along the edges. Then, gently shake the pan to release the egg from the bottom of the pan.

Grabbing the handle, tilt the pan forward and spoon hot butter or oil over the egg. Continue basting until the yolk and white are opaque, 1 to 2 minutes).

Remove the pan from the heat and let the egg rest for a few seconds. The white should be completely firm and the yolk very runny. Serve immediately.

Perfect Basmati Rice

MAKES ABOUT 3 CUPS [360 G]

1½ cups [300 g] basmati rice
2½ cups [600 ml] water
½ tsp salt
½ tsp olive oil

Rinse the rice in several changes of water, draining through a fine-mesh sieve.

Combine the drained rice and the water in a medium, heavy-bottomed saucepan and bring to a boil over medium-high heat. Add the salt and olive oil and stir well to incorporate. Cover, decrease the heat to low, then cook for 15 minutes.

Remove the pan from the heat, let sit, covered, an additional 10 minutes, then fluff with a fork and serve.

Perfect Black Rice

MAKES ABOUT 3 CUPS [360 G]

1½ cups [300 g] black rice
2¾ cups [660 ml] water
½ tsp salt
1 Tbsp unsalted butter

Rinse the rice in several changes of water, draining through a fine-mesh sieve. Combine the drained rice and the water in a medium heavy-bottomed saucepan and bring to a boil over medium-high heat. Add the salt and butter and stir well to incorporate. Cover, decrease the heat to low, then cook until most of the water is absorbed and the rice is tender, approximately 35 minutes.

Remove the pan from the heat, let sit, covered, an additional 10 minutes, then fluff with a fork and serve.

Perfect Brown Rice

MAKES ABOUT 3 CUPS [360 G]

1½ cups [300 g] long-grain brown rice
2½ cups [600 ml] water
½ tsp salt
½ Tbsp unsalted butter

Rinse the rice in several changes of water, draining through a fine-mesh sieve. Combine the drained rice and the water in a medium heavy-bottomed saucepan and bring to a boil over medium-high heat. Add salt and butter and stir well to incorporate. Cover, decrease the heat to low, then cook until most of the water is absorbed and the rice is tender, approximately 30 minutes.

Remove the pan from the heat, let sit, covered, an additional 10 minutes, then fluff with a fork and serve.

Founders of wellforculture.com

Manoomin Elk Meatballs

Well For Culture is an indigenous wellness initiative, co-founded in 2014 by Chelsey Luger (Anishinaabe/Lakota) and Anthony Thosh Collins (O'odham/Haudenosaunee/ Wa-Zha-Zhi). The mission of Well For Culture is multi-faceted. We research and disseminate relevant wellness knowledge from indigenous and western perspectives in order to dispel harmful myths and offer suggestions for improving our collective health in Native communities. We encourage all wellness seekers to recognize and apply indigenous-based wellness knowledge and healing methods. Our hope is to inspire all people—especially Native youth—to live a healthy, happy lifestyle by utilizing food as medicine, by exercising on our earth gym, and by connecting the mental-physical-spiritual-emotional facets of wellness for holistic well-being.

These meatballs are a hybridized modern recipe for the carnivorous types who love wild game. Elk has been a staple food for many different tribes across North America. Manoomin (wild rice) has been at the center of the Ojibwe food culture since time immemorial. Now you can enjoy both of these highly nutritious foods in one meal packed with ancestral flavors. The elk can be substituted with any wild game or other meat such as bison, venison, or grass-fed, non-antibiotic beef. Serve with a dark leafy green salad (made with dandelion greens or kale) and sliced avocado for a complete meal.

SERVES 4 TO 6

1 Tbsp olive oil
1 lb [453 g] ground elk
2 cups [350 g] cooked wild rice, preferably Ojibwe
2 organic, free-range eggs, lightly beaten
12 garlic cloves, minced
½ small red onion, minced
1 tsp kosher salt
1 tsp freshly ground black pepper
1 large handful pumpkin seeds

Preheat the oven to 400°F [200°C]. Coat a sheet pan with the olive oil.

Place the elk, rice, eggs, garlic, onion, salt, and pepper in a large bowl and mix well to combine. Shape the mixture into 1½ in [4 cm] meatballs (you should end up with about 16 meatballs) and space them evenly on the sheet pan. Bake until they're firm to the touch and no longer pink in the middle, 20 to 25 minutes. Transfer the meatballs to a serving platter and sprinkle with the pumpkin seeds. Serve immediately.

HOW FOOD CAN IMPACT COMMUNITIES

By Caleb Zigas, Executive Director of La Cocina

I first read about La Cocina in a job posting on Craigslist. This was the early 2000s and I was looking to transition from restaurant work into social justice, and the organization was looking for its leadership. Massively under-qualified, I applied nonetheless, and was roundly ignored, likely for good reason. But I snuck in as a volunteer, opening the doors to the San Francisco Mission District kitchen every morning at 6 AM, a vital, if tedious, responsibility. I was drawn to La Cocina because of a deep belief that everyone deserves an opportunity to make a living doing something that they love to do.

La Cocina was built to offer a space to address the problems that are evident right outside those very doors I opened. Each morning, on the way to work, I would pass dozens of men, mostly from Mexico and Central

America, waiting on the corner of 26th Street, looking to secure informal work in the day-laborer economy. A middle-aged woman on the same street would wheel a stroller full of still-hot Mexican empanadas and a cooler of arroz con leche that she would sell for a dollar. These were fried masa cakes stuffed with melty cheese (not the baked South American versions) and she covered them with chopped lettuce, sour cream, and salsa. They were perfect. The arroz con leche was piping hot and would stick to your throat when you could coax it out of the Styrofoam cup. I would get both every morning as did nearly every one of those men on the corner. She had, I realized, not only a thriving business but also a community-driven solution to a community-based need. That's what food can do. Cooking is not glamorous work, but feeding people will always offer a grander opportunity for community building.

La Cocina was born out of the belief that our cities can be better places. Across the country, informal economies sprout out of barriers to entry that we intentionally and unintentionally erect. These barriers discourage all kinds of entrepreneurs from ever pursuing their dreams. If you look hard enough, you will find these informal entrepreneurs everywhere. It's not just the woman selling empanadas, it's also the man selling barbecue out of the back of his truck in parking lots, the pop-up in the back of a bodega, the meal delivered to a high-rise apartment building, and the pies for sale on a country road. More than anything, the informal economy represents the search, quite an American one, for economic freedom.

Our economy, in particular our current, first-quarter, twenty-first-century economy, does not often offer opportunity graciously. After a severe recession, and amidst a recovery of the market threatened by automation and the unequal distribution of wealth and income, the working class has been particularly hard hit. And there are few industries more working class than the food industry.

We are all living at a time of unmatched economic inequality and great need. We honor chefs at restaurants where the four-hour tasting menu might be the equivalent of seventy-one hours of minimum-wage work. We fight for fifteen-dollar wages in front of companies that book billions of dollars in annual profits. We search high and low for delicious dumplings and tasty tacos in neighborhoods where for-profit developers are actively purchasing low-income housing and displacing the residents that made the neighborhoods neighborly in the first place.

On top of those challenges, the food industry has long been male dominated, with as much as 75 percent of business ownership in the hands of men, and an average of 73 cents for a woman's wages to a man's dollar across roles. Similarly, the food industry has exploited immigrant labor and that of communities of color, for nearly as long as it has been around, building business models that depend on the whims of customers (tipping) to meet living wages for front-of-the-house employees and advocating against an increased minimum wage that could change the economic landscape for the back of the house. Wealth and capital still continue to define the ways in which entrepreneurs bring their products to market, a reality that has particularly grave implications for black and immigrant communities who might aspire to business ownership in a market absent of investment.

Food is at the heart of all of this. And we can all be doing more to ensure that the food system that we live in, and thus the communities that we are building, are more equitable. We can, and must, create ownership opportunities for anyone who wants to spend their lives cooking food. We can offer to pay a little more for our food so that those who would cook the food might eat it, too. We can advocate for our communities to remain affordable so that we might welcome all kinds of people into those neighborhoods.

People sell food because people want to buy it. Demand drives marketplaces, and we all have an opportunity to shape the nature of the supply. A truly rational economy would adjust to that equation justly. Since that's not how our economy currently operates, we as citizens and communities must be compelled to act.

Food business ownership, despite all of these challenges, still offers one of the most fundamental routes to asset generation that our country has. And talented cooks, chefs, and entrepreneurs across the country are looking for their opportunity. We all have the tools to make those dreams a reality. La Cocina begins by understanding who the hidden entrepreneurs are, identifying the barriers to entry that exist in the marketplace, and then bridging the social and financial capital that is required to access those opportunities. This is work that can and does happen every day.

As we think about what we want the future of our cities, and our food world, to look like, we must consider equity and opportunity to be indivisible. The chefs hidden in plain sight in micro-communities across the country are the leaders and community builders that we need. That leadership begins with understanding the privilege and access that some in our industry have, and using those tools to expand access and open doors.

An oft-asked question in the food industry wonders what we, the privileged, can do to empower marginalized communities with access to opportunity. But the question itself, one that imagines power as a gift and not an asset, ignores how powerful these communities already are, how much these cooks accomplish on a daily basis. Instead, we have to look at what power we might be able to sacrifice, or what privilege we are willing to share.

La Cocina has incubated over thirty businesses into economic or operational self-sufficiency, and over twenty-three brick and mortar locations have opened, beginning with less than five thousand dollars in capital. The women who have launched businesses out of our incubator are leaders, both in the food industry and in their community at large. But they can't do this work by themselves. Community building requires the collective movement of the community, and we must all be engaged in setting the table that we hope to sit at. We have plenty of work to do, and we intend to be well fed while doing it.

Roasted Broccoli + Quinoa with Curry Cashew Dressing

This is such a simple vegan meal, but really nourishing and quite delicious. Each component (the roasted broccoli, quinoa, and cashew dressing) can be made in big batches and stored in airtight containers in the refrigerator for up to a week. That way you can assemble these bowls whenever you're hungry or use the components separately (use the cashew dressing as a dip for vegetables, make a roasted broccoli omelet, and treat the quinoa like rice and stir-fry it with peas, eggs, and soy sauce). Taking a little time to stock your fridge with healthy, homemade food is an act of self-care that will serve you well while you're busy resisting. In other words, it's important to take care of yourself so you can better take care of the world. Note that if you can only find roasted cashews that aren't salted, just season the dressing to taste with salt.

SERVES 4

1 lb [453 g] fresh broccoli, tough stems discarded,
   cut into large florets
2 Tbsp olive oil
1½ tsp kosher salt, divided
½ cup [65 g] roasted and salted cashews
2 tsp curry powder
3 Tbsp freshly squeezed lemon juice
2¼ cups [540 ml] water, divided
1 cup [180 g] quinoa

Preheat the oven to 425°F [220°C]. Place a sheet pan in the oven to heat up.

Meanwhile, place the broccoli in a large bowl, drizzle with the olive oil, and sprinkle with ½ tsp of the salt. Toss everything well to combine.

Once the oven comes to temperature, place the broccoli on the hot sheet pan in an even layer. Roast the broccoli, stirring it now and then, until it's softened, browned, and crisp on the edges, about 30 minutes total.

Meanwhile, place the cashews in a blender along with the curry powder, lemon juice, and ½ cup [120 ml] of the water. Blend until smooth and reserve the mixture.

Lastly, rinse the quinoa in a fine-mesh sieve and then place it in a medium saucepan set over high heat with the remaining 1 tsp salt and the remaining 1¾ cups [420 ml] water. Bring the mixture to a boil, decrease the heat, cover, and simmer until the quinoa has absorbed all of the water and is softened, about 12 minutes. Turn off the heat and put a kitchen towel between the pot and the lid and let the quinoa sit for 10 minutes (the towel will absorb excess steam). Uncover the quinoa, fluff it with a fork, and divide it among 4 serving bowls. Top with the roasted broccoli, and drizzle with the cashew dressing.

Serve immediately.

FROM JT

Greek Chickpea Salad

A cross between a Greek salad and a bean salad, this dish requires no actual cooking, just a bit of chopping and assembling. It's the perfect meal to make when you want something healthy but don't want to turn on the stove or spend more than 10 minutes at the counter (like, for example, when you're spending your lunch hour getting in touch with your representatives). It's also a testament to a can of chickpea's convenience, versatility, affordability, and healthiness. If you're vegan, simply omit the feta cheese. This salad is best enjoyed right after you make it when everything is crunchy and fresh, but it can absolutely hang out in a covered container in the refrigerator for up to 3 days without any worries. Serve over chopped arugula or romaine if you want a bit more heft. Toasted pita bread would be welcome, too.

SERVES 2 AS A MAIN DISH, 4 AS A SIDE DISH

2 Tbsp red wine vinegar
¼ cup [60 ml] olive oil
1 garlic clove, minced
½ tsp kosher salt, plus more as needed
1 tsp dried oregano, rubbed between your fingertips
One 15-oz [425-g] can chickpeas, rinsed and drained
1 medium English cucumber, ends trimmed, coarsely
  chopped

1 red, orange, or yellow bell pepper, stemmed, seeded, and coarsely chopped

½ small red onion, thinly sliced

2 large vine-ripened tomatoes, cored and cut into bite-size wedges (or 2 large handfuls cherry tomatoes, halved)

½ cup [60 g] crumbled feta cheese

½ cup [100 g] green or black olives

Place the vinegar, olive oil, garlic, salt, and oregano in a large bowl and whisk well to combine. Add the chickpeas, cucumber, bell pepper, onion, and tomatoes and mix gently to combine. Season the salad to taste with salt. Transfer it to a serving bowl or to individual bowls and top with the feta and olives.

Serve immediately.

Spicy Tandoori Cauliflower with Minted Yogurt

This incredibly flavorful cauliflower is one of my favorite vegetarian dishes since it's so filling. The yogurt and assertive spice combination give the cauliflower an enormous depth of flavor and a really rich texture. This also is incredibly easy to make and I love that you get to use the yogurt for both parts of the dish. If you want to save yourself some cleaning, line the hot sheet pan with parchment paper before you put the cauliflower on it. I find that you get less crispy bits when you do that, though, so I just soak the pan afterwards and call it a day. For a complete meal, serve this with white or brown rice, quinoa, or warm flatbread and a platter of sliced cucumbers that you've drizzled with lemon juice and sprinkled with salt.

SERVES 4

1 cup [227 g] full-fat Greek yogurt, divided
2 Tbsp olive oil
2 garlic cloves, minced
1 tsp ground turmeric
1 tsp ground cumin
½ tsp ground cayenne pepper
Kosher salt
1 lb [453 g] fresh cauliflower (about 1 medium), cut into large florets
2 Tbsp freshly squeezed lemon or lime juice
1 large handful fresh mint leaves, minced

Preheat the oven to 425°F [220°C]. Place a sheet pan in the oven to heat up.

Meanwhile, place ½ cup [113 g] of the yogurt in a large bowl with the olive oil, garlic, turmeric, cumin, cayenne, and ½ tsp of salt and whisk well to combine. Add the cauliflower and mix well so that each piece is coated.

Once the oven comes to temperature, place the cauliflower on the hot sheet pan in an even layer. Roast, stirring the cauliflower once or twice while it's in the oven, until it's softened and gorgeously browned, about 25 minutes total. Season the cauliflower to taste with salt.

Meanwhile, place the remaining ½ cup [113 g] yogurt in a small bowl with the lemon or lime juice, mint, and ½ tsp of salt and whisk well to combine.

Serve the cauliflower hot or at room temperature with the minted yogurt spooned on top.

GROUND RULES TO ORGANIZED ACTIVISM

By Callie Jayne, Lead Organizer, Citizen Action of New York

In this moment of the whirlwind, we are seeing a surge in activism, the type of activism where people—many for the first time—are engaged in trying to make real changes in their communities. Many people are angry or scared, and we are seeing increased mobilization of members of the community to address local, state, and federal issues. But hyper-vigilance and mass mobilization without strategy is a sure way to wear us all down. We must use our energy strategically in order to achieve the type of world that we all believe is possible.

As a community organizer, my role is to organize the community, to provide the skill and strategy necessary to make changes in our community. How do we bring together many people to fight toward common goals?

We bring people together with some basic ground rules.

ASSUME BEST INTENTIONS – Create a space where people feel safe to make a mistake. We are all on a journey and we should assume that people are trying their best.

ONE MICROPHONE – Whoever is loudest is often most heard, but now we must let all people speak, and be heard. Whoever is holding the microphone is the only one who should be speaking.

PROGRESSIVE STACK – Pay attention to those who don't often get to speak: call on people who aren't often heard (people of color, LGBTQ people, and women) before those who are. Move these voices to the top of the stack.

NON-MARTIAN CLAUSE – Speak in a way that can engage all people in the room, avoiding acronyms, jargon, or elitist language. Be willing to explain to people who don't understand.

Basic ground rules like these help to bring together all types of people, and allow us to build our collective strength by developing a shared understanding. A shared understanding allows us to work together to do meaningful work.

Being strategic in organizing is the only way to win. Strategy involves a series of long-term,

46

intermediary, and short-term goals. Each goal needs a target, a person who has the power to get you what you want, or stop what you don't want to happen. Organized Activism is putting aside your emotions, and understanding the bigger picture.

The bigger picture addresses all three levels of power. The first level is immediate and focuses on changing laws and policies, impacting elections, and impacting political decisions. Activists spend a lot of time working on this level fighting the thing, fighting for the thing, and fighting against the thing. This work is important, it impacts people, but we can't just live here. The second level is building deeper infrastructure, the grass roots. We need to build enough power in our community to make the changes that we want to make in the world. We need to empower the most impacted people on these issues and shift the power dynamic. The third and largest level is all about changing the worldview. All three levels must be balanced in order to be effective and achieve the goals that we hope to achieve.

We have to stop looking at each single fight. We need to start looking at what type of world we want to see. Each decision must be building the movement, every tactic must be taking us closer to our goal.

We have to be smart. We have to be strong. We have to be open to learn. We have to be willing to listen. We can win, but we must be organized.

Thai Yellow Curry Vegetable Pot

Healthy and nourishing, this flexible and completely vegan recipe is the answer to all the random vegetables kicking around your refrigerator and counter. As long as you add them to the pot in whatever order they cook in (hard vegetables first, leafy ones last), you'll be good to go. My favorite brand of curry paste is Mae Ploy, but use whatever you can find (Thai Kitchen and Roland are also good brands). You can of course make your own, but store-bought curry paste makes this super fast and easy.

SERVES 4

2 Tbsp olive oil

2 large shallots or 1 small red onion, finely chopped

2 Tbsp minced peeled fresh ginger

4 garlic cloves, minced

3 Tbsp Thai yellow curry paste

One 13.5-oz [398-g] can coconut milk (full-fat or low-fat, up to you)

Kosher salt

2 lb [906 g] any and all vegetables, cut into bite-size pieces

Cooked rice or rice noodles (optional)

Cilantro, chopped peanuts or cashews, lime wedges, chile paste, and a bottle of fish sauce or Bragg Liquid Aminos for serving

Place the olive oil in a large pot set over medium-high heat. Add the shallots, ginger, and garlic and cook, stirring now and then, until barely softened, about 2 minutes. Add the curry paste and stir well to lightly fry the paste and just wake it up, about 30 seconds. Add the coconut milk and whisk well to dissolve the curry paste. Increase the heat to high and let it come to a boil and then decrease the heat to a simmer. Season the mixture to taste with salt (the amount will depend on your curry paste, but figure about 1 tsp). Stir in any hard vegetables that take a while to cook (chopped carrots, cabbage, and/or potatoes all come to mind), cover the pot, and let them simmer until they're tender, about 10 minutes. Stir in any vegetables that just take a little bit to get tender (things like trimmed green beans, sliced peppers, and broccoli) and let them cook, covered, until tender, about 5 minutes. Lastly stir in any vegetables that need to just be kissed by the heat (frozen peas, snow peas, baby spinach, shredded kale) and cook them until they're tender, about 2 minutes. Give everything a nice stir and season to taste with salt.

Serve straight from the pot with rice or rice noodles if you'd like. Put out bowls of cilantro, peanuts or cashews, and lime wedges, plus bottles of chile paste and fish sauce or Bragg Liquid Aminos so everyone can top their bowl to their liking.

Sheet Pan Sausage, Potatoes + Red Cabbage

This is the simplest, easiest, and most comforting meal and gives you the satisfaction of meat and potatoes without much work or money. It's the ideal thing to just throw in the oven while you're doing a bunch of other things (say organizing a box of books by undervalued authors of color to donate to your local library . . . or reading one yourself). Feel free to use whatever type of fresh sausage you like and you can swap green cabbage or halved Brussels sprouts for the red cabbage and also use diced sweet potatoes, parsnips, and/or carrots instead of the small white potatoes. Serve with jars of Dijon mustard and prepared horseradish.

SERVES 4

1 lb [453 g] red cabbage, cored and thinly sliced (about ½ small head)

1½ lb [680 g] small white creamer potatoes, halved (or Yukon gold potatoes cut into bite-size pieces)

3 Tbsp olive oil

1 tsp kosher salt

8 fresh sweet and/or hot Italian sausages (about 2 lb [906 g] total)

Small handful finely chopped fresh parsley leaves

Preheat the oven to 375°F [190°C].

Place the cabbage and potatoes on a sheet pan. Drizzle with the olive oil, sprinkle with the salt, and mix everything together with your hands, spreading it out so that the vegetables are in an even layer. Roast the vegetables until just beginning to soften, about 25 minutes. Prick the sausages in a couple of places (to let the steam escape) and evenly space them on top of the vegetables. Roast until the sausages are cooked through, the potatoes are tender, and the cabbage is wilted, 25 more minutes. Sprinkle the parsley on top and serve directly from the sheet pan.

FEEDING THE MASSES:

YUM!

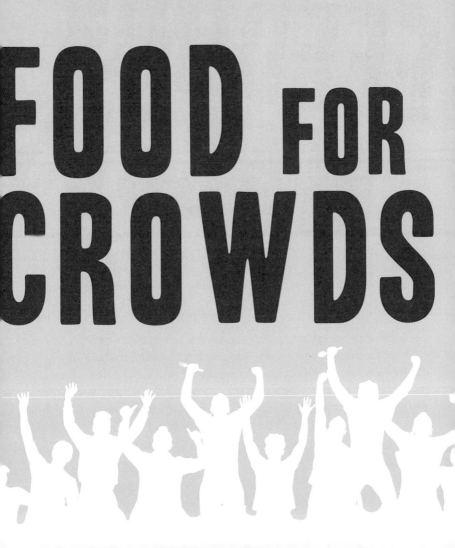

FOOD FOR CROWDS

Dark Roux Mushroom Gumbo

When making this gumbo, it is important to remember two things: A clean, homemade vegetable stock makes all the difference in the world. And a "dark" roux is essential for getting the deep, rich flavor that is the hallmark of Louisiana gumbos. The combination of freshly made stock and slow-simmered roux will guarantee a party-pleasing dish that will have your folks coming back for seconds and thirds.

If you aren't familiar with classic Louisiana cooking, roux—a combination of equal parts flour and fat—is the foundation of a tasty gumbo. In addition to adding bold flavor to gumbos, roux serves as a thickener (cooking it over low heat removes the flour's raw taste). Typically, all-purpose flour is used to make a classic roux, but I have been working on a gluten-free roux for months, and I finally struck gold. I find that millet flour not only works well as a substitute for wheat, but also gives the roux a nutty flavor that further emboldens the taste of the overall dish. To be clear, there is no getting around the time-consuming nature of roux preparation. This one requires over an hour of stirring, so grab a bottle of wine, recruit a few friends to help (take turns every 15 minutes), and do dat. Note: millet flour does not turn as dark (chocolate) as roux made with wheat flour, but you will know your roux is ready when it is the color of a roasted chickpea.

This gumbo will easily feed full servings to 6 to 8 people, but if it is being served as a part of a larger spread, it can easily feed more. Enjoy along with rice, baaaaaby.

SERVES 6 TO 8

Extra-virgin olive oil
½ lb [227 g] shiitake mushrooms, stems discarded, caps sliced ¼ in [6 mm] thick
½ lb [227 g] cremini mushrooms, sliced ¼ in [6 mm] thick
Fine sea salt
1 lb [453 g] portobello mushrooms, sliced ½ in [12 mm] thick
¾ cup [55 g] millet flour
½ small yellow onion, chopped into ¼-in [6-mm] dice
2 stalks celery, chopped into ¼-in [6-mm] dice
½ large green bell pepper, stemmed, seeded, and chopped into ¼-in [6-mm] dice
2 garlic cloves, minced
6 cups [1.4 L] vegetable stock, at room temperature
2 Tbsp tamari
2 bay leaves
Pinch of ground cayenne pepper
1 lb [453 g] Swiss chard, stemmed and coarsely chopped
5 Tbsp [12 g] fresh thyme leaves
Freshly ground white pepper
Cooked rice for serving
6 large green onions, finely chopped
Filé powder for garnishing

In a large cast-iron skillet, heat 1 Tbsp of oil. Add the shii-take mushroom slices, cover, and cook over medium heat, stirring occasionally, until fork-tender, 5 to 7 minutes. Transfer the mushrooms to a bowl and set aside.

Next, heat 2 Tbsp of oil in the skillet, add the cremini mushroom slices in a single layer, and cook over high heat, without stirring, until most of the liquid has evaporated and the mushrooms start to brown, 2 to 3 minutes. Turn each mushroom slice with a fork and cook for an additional 1 to 2 minutes, until browned. Transfer to the bowl of shiitakes, sprinkle with a large pinch of salt, and stir to evenly coat.

Line a plate with paper towels and set nearby. Pour enough oil in the skillet to coat the bottom of the pan. Without overcrowding, add as many of the portobello mushroom slices to cover the pan and cook over high heat until golden brown, about 2 minutes. Turn each mushroom slice and cook for an additional 1 to 2 minutes, until browned. Trans-fer the mushrooms onto the prepared plate and sprinkle with salt on both sides. Do this in batches, adding more oil when necessary, until all the mushrooms are seared.

Over medium-high heat, add ½ cup [120 ml] of oil to the skillet and warm until shimmering. Slowly whisk in the flour, a little at a time, until mixed well, then stir frequently with a wooden spoon. When the mixture is slowly bubbling, decrease the heat to low. Cook the roux, stirring frequently to prevent burning, until it turns the color of a roasted chickpea and has a nutty aroma, about 1¼ hours. Add the onion, celery, and bell pepper, stir until well incorporated, and cook, stirring occasionally, until the vegetables start to soften, about 5 minutes. Add the garlic and cook for an additional 3 minutes.

Remove the roux-vegetable mixture from the heat. Transfer the contents with a rubber spatula to a large heavy-bottomed pot or a Dutch oven. Quickly whisk in all the vegetable stock and increase the heat to high, whisking the mixture until it comes to a boil. Add the tamari, bay leaves, cayenne, and 1 tsp of salt. Decrease the heat to medium-low and simmer for about 45 minutes.

While the gumbo is simmering, bring a large pot of water to a boil. Add 1 tsp of salt and the chard, bring back to a boil, and cook for 30 seconds. Quickly remove the chard with a slotted spoon or a spider and set aside.

Add the reserved shiitake and cremini mushrooms to the gumbo, and simmer for 5 minutes, stirring occasionally.

Stir 3 Tbsp of the thyme into the gumbo and simmer for an additional 3 minutes. Season to taste with salt and white pepper.

Serve the gumbo in shallow bowls over rice, add a few slices of the seared portobellos on top, and garnish with the remaining 2 Tbsp thyme, green onions, and filé powder. Place the blanched chard on the table for folks to add to their bowls for freshness and a pop of color.

FOOD IS LIKE SEX. IT IS THE PROVOCATION.

By Tunde Wey, Writer/Cook

Food is like sex. Food is also very different from sex, but only their similarities are particularly interesting right now.

So, food is like sex: both self-contained actions. Both are means to ends.

Sex, in the carnal moments of union, ending in an orgasmic clasp and shudders, is at times physical and definite; all that is being explored and satisfied is confined to the particular place and time of the consummation. Food, devoured gently or roughly scarfed, in many iterations is also about satiating basic biological imperatives, the degrees of deliciousness aiding the process.

Sex borrows from lust, which borrows from wonder. And wonder impels travel, peripateticism—one wanders to seek new and exciting things. This is the promiscuous nature of sex, the vow to explore a partner as an intimate way to experience what is otherwise closed off.

Food has a promiscuous, voyeuristic dimension as well. It can be used and misused as a tool to investigate the multifarious realities that exist outside our bubbles. We can traverse temporal, spatial constraints, and transcend corporeal phenomena to enter a place we never knew, the experience of the other. This is food as an object of the spirit, food at its best.

When sex is used as a spiritual object, it fully encompasses its Manichean possibilities of craven and curious. And food, in its most transcendent iteration, is a provocation for more. Once the body has belched, the spirit is summoned and we can engage in deeper intimacy, pillow talk, or dinner talk.

Lest we forget, the best make-up sex leads to actual making up apart from the sex. The act of sex does not a makeup make, unless literally and narrowly where it is makeup, a temporary cover to mask blemishes.

The real moment of glory in sex is the space it can create for intimate and vulnerable connection. It is not the opening act, it sets the stage for the next act, it is the stage on which individual and honest truths, sometimes opposing, meet and do the dance of realization. The stage must be sturdy. The bed should hold up all the lovers in safety.

The food is the stage, and it requires care and consideration in its construction to help fulfill the mission of intimacy. It must be delicious, force the partakers to lick their fingers, even lick off the fingers of the other, draw them closer, nearer to each other. When there is nothing left they are forced to stare into themselves and begin the difficult conversations.

Food is the intermediary, the intercessor, the patron saint of gentle and difficult exploration. We cannot forget this. The work of food then is to quietly exit, fade back into the background, permitting the players at the dinner table an attempt at understanding, at pillow talk.

But food is only the provocation, not a guarantee of change. This provocation doesn't just summon itself into being. It has to be coaxed out. It is not enough for food to be present, at least three master strokes are required to get the best from a meal, to spur the provocation that we hope eventually leads to transformation.

The first and the Lord of all things is discomfort. We must accept discomfort at the table, not the metaphorical sort, but the honest-to-goodness disconcerting variety. Discomfort produces doubt, it sets its gaze on our certainties and denies them vigorously. Doubt is the precursor to most new revelations and through our revelations we can produce astonishing actions.

We have to sit in the discomfort allowing it to tear us apart, tear us from the inside, poison our prejudices, drown our former selves. At the dinner table, after the beautiful things have been set in front of us, after we have had the first few bites, sipped a few sups, rubbed our bellies in contentment, we must bring the difficult matters to the fore. Without varnish, raw and unflinching, and discuss.

The second stroke? Remember the danger of false empathy!

We are only available to inhabit our own bodies and experiences and our peculiar circumstances prevent us from fully understanding a different perspective. At the dinner table, this sacred space of reconciliation, we must stifle the urge to understand other people's particular pain through our own perceived pain—they are different and not coequal.

Instead listen. Hold a space for others to be vulnerable, it is their space, do not compete for it with your story.

Third, we must maintain emotional proximateness to what's happening at the dinner table. In the face of discomfort our instinct is to flee or retreat, avoiding our own reflections.

Sometimes silence is fleeing: it is our perfect barrier, protecting against the onslaught of the break. Other times we flee with words that pull us away from the intimate moment. Afraid to be present in the uncomfortable space, we offer stories from the past or other people's stories, or both.

At the dinner table, we should be present, only speaking to our experience and preferably in the context of the present.

Let me add a fourth stroke: Work. Work. Work. Work. Work. If discomfort is the beginning of the journey, then emotional labor is the transportive element. We move along this axis of transformation powered only by the emotional work we are willing to do. The more work we do the steadier we go, and when we're sputtering or stalling, we probably aren't working. Transformation begins when we understand that we are not the protagonists. That moment when we perceive ourselves as oppressor and victimizer is the instance of true vulnerability, honest empathy, and deep discomfort, because we have ceased to externalize the problem.

The world will seldom change until we change, and we cannot change ourselves if we're unwilling to be deeply uncomfortable, do the emotional work necessary, and deny ourselves false empathy. If we are to do this difficult work, why not over delicious food and heartening drink?

Adobo sa Gata

It's not a coincidence that my pop-up dinner series is called
SALO, which is short of "Salu-salo," a Tagalog word which
means "gathering" or "dinner party." All of my dinners are
communal and food is meant to be shared with others at
the table.

Filipino culture centers around dining. Food always
brings people together. Whether you're a family of four or
ten, one always, and I mean always, cooks for 10 or more,
just in case a friend, a cousin, or a neighbor shows up at
your dinner table unannounced. If not, you can always eat
the leftovers the next day as "baon" (Tagalog for "prepped
meal to go").

This recipe is super-essential to me and my heritage,
mainly because it's dubbed as our national dish. This dish
was originally introduced by the Spanish colonizers, but it
has been adapted to the tropical islands. "Adobo" applies
to any meat that has been cooked with vinegar or acidity.
Back in the day, the Philippines didn't have any refriger-
ation, so they've made up dishes that could sustain their
flavor and quality without it. They use natural preservatives
such as sugar, vinegar, pepper, and soy sauce to make this
quintessential dish. It's a simple dish that can feed multitudes, and the best part is that it gets better the longer it
stays marinating in the sauce it's been cooked in. Adobo

sa Gata (Adobo with Coconut Milk) is from a region in the south of the Philippines, called Mindanao, where coconuts are bountiful.

SERVES 5
(TO SCALE UP FOR 20, MULTIPLY MEASUREMENTS BY 4)

1 cup [240 ml] spiced cane, white distilled, or
   rice wine vinegar
1 cup [240 ml] soy sauce
½ cup [120 ml] coffee
¼ cup [50 g] dark brown sugar
2 Tbsp coconut oil
2 heads of garlic, crushed and roughly chopped
2 medium shallots, diced
2 lbs [910 g] pork butt or belly, cut into 2-in [5-cm] cubes,
   fat included
2 Tbsp black peppercorns
10 bay leaves
1 lb [455 g] shiitake mushrooms, caps only, sliced thinly
6 oz [170 g] wood ear mushrooms, sliced
1 cup [240 ml] coconut cream
Cooked white rice, for serving

In a small bowl, combine the vinegar, soy, coffee, and sugar. Whisk to dissolve the sugar.

In a saucepan, heat the coconut oil over high heat. Add the garlic and shallots and cook, stirring constantly, until the shallots are clear and the garlic has browned, about 5 minutes. Add the pork and sear the fatty sides. Add the vinegar mixture, the peppercorns, and the bay leaves. Bring to a boil.

Decrease the heat to low, cover the pot, and simmer until the pork is fork-tender, 45 minutes to an hour. Stir in the shiitake and wood ear mushrooms and the coconut cream. Cover and simmer for 15 to 20 minutes more. Serve with white rice.

Brazilian Fish Potpie

I am always interested in exploring cuisines from the African Diaspora. When I travel to various countries (especially those with a strong diaspora population), I'm always amazed at how many aspects of the regions' cuisine can be traced back to Africa. This wonderment also stems from a certain pride I feel in knowing that in spite of the unspeakable cruelty that has been endured by my ancestors during the transatlantic slave trade to the Americas and the outlying islands, the historical and cultural elements in various dishes haven't been completely lost. From the Friday Night Fish Fry of the Deep South to the Poisson Yassa of Senegal, there is something special about a hearty and filling fish dish that binds us all in a beautiful way.

SERVES 16

PIECRUST

6 cups [720 g] unbleached all-purpose flour, plus more as needed for rolling

2 Tbsp granulated sugar

2 Tbsp kosher salt

1 lb [453 g] unsalted butter, cut in ½-in [1¼-cm] cubes and frozen for 15 minutes

About 1 cup [240 ml] ice water

FISH

1 cup [240 ml] distilled white vinegar

12 garlic cloves, crushed

2 tsp granulated sugar

1 Tbsp freshly ground black pepper

1 Tbsp ground coriander

1 Tbsp ground cumin

1 Tbsp red pepper flakes

1½ tsp ground turmeric

1½ tsp kosher salt

3 lb [1.3 kg] boneless, skinless white fish (such as 6 fillets of cod, whiting, haddock, or similar)

FILLING

3 Tbsp unsalted butter

3 Tbsp olive oil

3 large sweet onions, diced

1½ tsp kosher salt, plus more if needed

3 Tbsp granulated sugar, divided

¼ cup [60 ml] apple cider (or Mexican coke)

½ cup [60 g] unbleached all-purpose flour

4¼ cups [1 L] clam juice

2 large red bell peppers, stemmed, seeded, and diced

2 large green bell peppers, stemmed, seeded, and diced

1½ tsp ground coriander

1½ tsp ground turmeric

1½ tsp ground cumin

2 tsp red pepper flakes

1 Tbsp freshly ground black pepper

1 fresh jalapeño chile, stemmed, seeded, and diced
3½ cups [612 g] cooked long-grain rice (brown or white)
1 large egg, beaten

To make the crust, place the flour, sugar, and salt in a large bowl and whisk together. After 15 minutes, remove the butter from the freezer and cut it into the flour. Make sure the butter is integrated in the flour but there are still large cubes of butter available throughout the mixture. Use your hands to do this or a pastry cutter. This will give us marbles of butter in our crust and ensure that the crust will be flaky. Slowly add the ice water, ¼ cup [60 ml] at a time, to the dry mixture and mix just until the dough comes together (you might not need all of the water). With your hands, knead the pastry until it's no longer dry, just about 1 minute. The pastry should feel malleable, but not "doughy." If the dough is too soft, you've added too much water and will need to add more flour. Divide the dough in half and form each into a disk. Wrap each disk with plastic wrap. Pop it in the fridge so that it can rest and chill for at least 30 minutes and up to 24 hours.

For the fish, place the vinegar, garlic, sugar, the black pepper, coriander, cumin, red pepper flakes, turmeric, and salt in a large bowl and whisk together. Place the mixture in a large resealable plastic bag and add the fish; use your hands to make sure the marinade touches all of the fish. Place the bag in the refrigerator for 1 hour, flipping it once.

For the rest of the filling, place the butter and olive oil in a large pot set over medium heat. Once the butter melts, add the onions. Cook, stirring now and then, until the onions are translucent and are starting to brown, about 12 minutes. Add the salt and 1½ Tbsp of the sugar and cook, stirring now and then, until the onions are deep golden brown, about 5 minutes. Add the apple cider and cook until the liquid is evaporated, about 2 minutes. Take the pot off the heat and add the flour and stir until all of the onions are coated with the flour. Return the pot to the heat and add the clam juice. Stir well while the mixture cooks to dissolve the flour. Cook until the mixture is slightly thickened, about 5 minutes, and then stir in the red and green peppers. Season the mixture to taste with more salt as needed.

Remove the fish from the marinade (discard the marinade) and add it to the pot. Press the fish down into the mixture so that it's submerged and cook just until the fish begins to flake, about 5 minutes. Stir with a wooden spoon to break the fish into smaller pieces. Add the remaining 1½ Tbsp of sugar, the coriander, turmeric, cumin, red pepper flakes, black pepper, jalapeño, and rice and stir well to combine. Remove the pot from the stove and season the mixture to taste with salt. Let the mixture cool to room temperature.

Preheat the oven to 365°F [185°C] . Line the middle rack of your oven with a piece of aluminum foil that's larger than a 12-by-17-in [30-by-43-cm] rimmed baking sheet to catch any inevitable drips from the pie when it bakes.

Roll out both chilled pie dough disks on a lightly floured work surface so that they're each slightly larger than a 12-by-17-in [30-by-43-cm] rimmed baking sheet. This will leave enough dough to come up and hang over the sides. Place one sheet of dough on a rimmed baking sheet and make sure it comes all the way up all of the sides. Top with the fish filling. Cover the filling with the second rolled-out pie dough and pinch or crimp the edges of the top and bottom crusts together to seal. Using a small paring knife, cut a dozen vents in the top of the piecrust so that steam can escape. Place the beaten egg in a small bowl with 1 Tbsp of water and whisk together. Brush the top of the dough with the egg wash (discard any extra). Place the baking sheet directly on top of the foil on the oven rack. Bake the pie until the crust is golden brown and the filling bubbles, about 1 hour.

Let the pie cool for at least 10 minutes before slicing and serving.

HAWA HASSAN

CEO, Basbaas Sauce

Suugo: The Somali Pasta Sauce

The very name of this recipe suggests the richness and diversity that goes into its makeup. Somali food is typically seasoned with a spice blend called xawaash (pronounced hawash), and it helps give every recipe a unique level of flavoring. I grew up with it, adore it, and personalize it in every way I can. I also come from a family with ten children, and like so many others I can attest to the appeal of a good pasta with a great pasta sauce. That's what we get with this concoction—a tasty blend that's easy to create and keeps a big family happy. In many versions of this dish you'll find beef as the protein of choice. I go a different way with turkey, which can be quite bland in some settings, but becomes a strong addition here.

SERVES 8

XAWAASH
½ cup [70 g] cumin seeds
½ cup [80 g] coriander seeds
2 Tbsp black peppercorns
One 2-in [5-cm] piece cinnamon stick
6 cardamom pods
1 tsp whole cloves
2 Tbsp ground turmeric

½ cup [120 ml] olive oil
1 red onion, finely chopped
1 green bell pepper, stemmed, seeded, and finely chopped
4 garlic cloves, minced
2 lb [1 kg] ground turkey
2 Tbsp xawaash
2 tsp kosher salt, plus more if needed
Two 28-oz [794-g] cans diced tomatoes
2 Tbsp tomato paste
2 Tbsp finely chopped fresh cilantro leaves
1 tsp freshly ground black pepper

Cooked pasta for serving

To make the xawaash, place the cumin and coriander seeds, black peppercorns, cinnamon, cardamom pods, and cloves in a skillet set over medium heat. Cook, stirring, until the spices are very fragrant, about 1½ minutes. Transfer the spices to a plate and let them cool to room temperature. Once cooled, transfer the spices to a clean coffee grinder and pulse until finely ground. If needed, sift the mixture and then regrind any coarse spices. Place the ground spices in a bowl and add the turmeric and whisk to combine. Store the mixture in an airtight jar in a dark spot at room temperature.

To make the suugo, place the olive oil, onion, green pepper, and garlic in a large skillet set over medium-high heat.

Cook, stirring now and then, until the vegetables begin to soften, about 8 minutes. Add the turkey, xawaash, and salt and cook, stirring now and then to break up the turkey, until the meat is browned, about 15 minutes.

Add the diced tomatoes (and their juice) and the tomato paste and stir well to combine, being sure to scrape up any bits stuck to the bottom of the skillet. Increase the heat to high and bring the sauce to a boil, then decrease the heat to low and simmer for 30 minutes. Stir now and then while the sauce cooks. Turn off the heat and stir in the cilantro and pepper.

Season to taste with salt and serve hot over cooked pasta.

DEVITA DAVISON

Executive Director, FoodLab Detroit

Southern-Style Boiled Cabbage with Smoked Turkey

I personally believe that the rest of the country is just now catching up to what Southerners have known for decades. That we can grow our food as an act of independence from, and resistance to, an unjust food system that is structurally racist, economically oppressive, and environmentally toxic.

My parents were born in Alabama, raised on farms that were owned by their families for generations. In my family our meals were born off farms and gardens. And I believe that in everything tied to creating great food and memorable experiences, there's a human touch. The touch of life—hands tenderly kneading biscuit dough, snapping beans, shucking corn, cutting cabbage, and shelling peas—is what makes Southern food expressive and intimate, attributes that are unattainable in mass-produced foods.

I can vividly recall traditional Southern feasts—picnics, church revival dinners, and homecoming celebrations—where my grandmother, mother, and aunts filled the long tables with side dishes like field peas, string beans, fried corn, succotash, and my mother's "world famous" Southern-style cabbage. My mother has quite a reputation for making the best cabbage and she would prepare 20 to 30 pounds of the delicacy for folks to take home. Even as a young girl, I knew my mother's cabbage was something coveted. People would ask, "Who made the cabbage?" And if the answer wasn't Martha Davison, they'd skip the dish.

SERVES 12

2 smoked turkey butts (or wings), rinsed
4 lb [1.8 kg] green cabbage (about 2 medium heads), sliced
2 tsp kosher salt
1 Tbsp granulated sugar
1 garlic clove, peeled and left whole
1 medium onion, peeled and left whole
1 Tbsp vegetable oil
1 small piece hot chile pepper

Place 2 qt [2 L] water and the turkey butts in a large pot set over medium-high heat. Bring the mixture to a boil and let the turkey boil for 1 hour. Keep adding water as it boils to keep the level the same. Add the cabbage, salt, sugar, garlic, onion, vegetable oil, and hot pepper to the pot and cook slowly until the cabbage is tender, 40 minutes. Do not overcook.

Serve hot.

HOW FOOD CAN BE A PLATFORM FOR ACTIVISM

By Shakirah Simley, Co-Founder and Organizer, Nourish/
Resist

I am having "the talk" with my younger brother.

Sunday afternoons are sibling time. We chose Thai.
The gracious staff, glossy pictorial menus, and leftover-
friendly portions make for a welcome compromise.
Dishes are unpronounceable because of a language
barrier, not the obscure naming conventions of a tattoo-
clad chef. The price of rice does not induce sticker shock.
I won't side-eye his sweet tooth ("Yes, a Thai iced tea,
please. And the fried banana with ice cream, thank you")
and he won't tell mom about my daytime Singha.

We are far from the "Asian cuisine" of our child-
hood. Where fluorescent-lit, faded menus highlight
specialties for a faraway banquet, not meant for us.
Where greasy paper bags of deep-fried chicken wings
were shoved through bulletproof-glass windows. Where

the lone, sticky tabletop was never enticing enough to stay, unless you had no place to call home. Where we could feed six rumbling bellies for twelve dollars. Where the seething racial strife between poor folks erupted into arguments about miscounted change, missing duck sauce packets, or murmured epithets.

We, however, dined with a familiar unease.

"I know you know what to do, but can we review? Please?" My tone belied a bit more panic than I intended.

"Okay, Kirah." The impatient tap of his chopsticks, grasping elusive chunks of barbecued pork, punctuate my sisterly lecture.

"Don't make eye contact with the officer in the first place. Stay calm. Don't raise my voice. Keep my hands where they can see them. Have my ID close by. Blah, blah, blah I get it, alright?"

I hated how well he wore his resignation. Three days prior, we watched on Facebook Live as Philando Castile bled to death in his car, shot five times by a police officer outside St. Paul, Minnesota. His girlfriend, Diamond Reynolds, in a surreal state of distressed composure, captured the extrajudicial killing and even corrected the officer's attempt to "reframe" the shooting. "Stay with me," she trembles. "We got pulled over for a busted taillight in the back." Thirty-six hours before Diamond lost Philando, Alton Sterling was gunned down in Baton Rouge by a white Louisiana police officer while selling CDs outside a convenience store. We watched over a grainy cell phone video, as he is shot at point blank range while lying on the ground. Alton was the one hundred eighty-fourth black person to be killed by police that year. Footage of his murder and similar incidents had been captured and shared increasingly online, making the daily slaughter of black people by police America's new prurient pastime, for even the casual social media user.

This year, I decided to add something new to the conversation.

"If you see a bystander, call out to them. Ask them to film your interaction on their phone."

With a quick bite of khao pad, he says, rather flatly, "Filming is not going to save my life, Kirah."

I am still broken from his comment. My little brother, who always carries the heaviest bag for me as we walk home from the grocery store, who can identify car engines based on their whisper or roar, and who tucks his lanky arms into slim-fit denim jackets (his preference over basketball jerseys). My little brother who always looks over his shoulder on his way home at night, keeps an ear out for a curt police siren and warning lights, and thinks twice before donning a dark-colored hoodie. It's as if his twenty-three years are just borrowed time.

As a black woman, I cannot explain to non-People of Color the sort of painful, racial trauma that constantly makes you mourn for something that has already occurred (e.g., the deaths of Oscar Grant, Philando Castile, Alton Sterling, Eric Garner, Rekia Boyd), and grieve for something that may, inevitably, happen (e.g., the future harm or murder of your brother or sister). This is the real terror in all of this. We're limiting the physical freedom of black and brown people, but also their childhoods, their sense of self and security, and literal futures.

As a food activist, I can explain to fellow advocates that our accountability to human beings presupposes our commitment to local food chains, organic produce, and craft production. Our collective resistance cannot be disavowed from the brutal history and experience of oppressed people. To do so would be to plan for a harvest, ignoring what you've sown.

Prioritizing racial equity within the good food movement requires an intentional shift from the dis-heartening spectrum of white responses to the racial realities of People of Color (POC). From the insidious sting of passive indifference, to hefty white savior complexes, to culturally appropriative recipes and restau-rants, to the straight-up exploitation of black and brown bodies, such responses do not engender trust of folks of color toward their white counterparts. It's one thing to show up and protest. It's another to ask "Why are you really here? And for whom?"

Our multiracial movement building needs to be fueled by reconciliation and atonement. Food spaces and food people are unique champions to create room for, and facilitate, this healing. Unpacking this racial trauma is best served over warming bowls of peppery oxtail stew or silky dhansak. These conversations should occur everywhere and all the time, particularly in school cafeterias, food pantries, church kitchens, public parks, and at dining room tables. And white people will have to examine themselves, and with each other first; unexamined privilege is a conditional dinner invite.

Creating anti-racist food spaces to dismantle white supremacy and patriarchy is a nourishing, worthwhile endeavor, with a few ground rules to start:

Our Care Has Multitudes. We can care about multiple things at the same time. A conversation on race is not a distraction from, say, the fight to change federal school lunch policies. An intersectional approach requires that we acknowledge the different ways in which systemic oppression harms folks based on their multiple identities. Therefore, the experiences and everyday worry of women, immigrants, POCs, queer, and trans folk can and should inform our work and priorities in the good food movement.

Educate Yourself. External organizing takes internal work and personal accountability and education. This work will be painful. Take the time to learn and honor people of color, past and present, who have toiled for racial justice, without their emotional labor or heavy lifting.

Decolonize Decision-Making. Creating space for resistance and reconciliation requires POC leadership from the start, from menu planning to choosing spaces, designing meal service to conversation facilitation. Resist good white intentions for the sake of POC mutual consent, trust, and ownership to foster safe, welcoming experiences for everyone.

Shift or Step Back. Power paradigms exist within institutions and individual conversations. Simple tactics, including listening to listen, taking up less space with one's feelings of guilt and shame, avoiding microaggressions, prioritizing "solutions" over process, are necessary for constructive dialogue. Prioritize non-hegemonic, non-white experiences.

Recognize the Debt. Acknowledge the ways that you have benefited from your social status, even if you didn't ask for it or earn it. From the land one occupies or farms, to food culture co-opted for cool points, to the fresh produce on our plates, it's likely that privilege sits on the backs of exploited folks of color. Any anti-racist conversation or space must start from this recognition.

Become an Accomplice, Not an Ally. Accomplices willingly accept the consequences and risk associated with collective liberation, whether emotional, financial, or physical. Allies center themselves and intentions in resistance work, comfortably and temporarily, behind battle lines. This work must be done side by side with unrelenting and fierce solidarity, weaponizing privilege and understanding that true justice comes with civil disobedience.

In my work, we seek to nourish so that we may resist. An intersectional approach to our good food work will require a new level of accountability and difficult conversations among our movement. I'm tired of having "the talk" with my little brother. But hopefully, with these meaningful, action-oriented conversations around the dinner table, I won't have them with my son.

STEPHEN SATTERFIELD

Writer, Speaker, Multimedia Producer, Founder of Whetstone

Baked Japanese Sweet Potatoes, Oven-Roasted Tomato Sauce, and Baked Polenta

A.K.A. A Resistance Meal for the Masses on the Simple and Cheap

Feeding lots of people is one of the reasons I first became interested in food. For those of us who speak our love through cooking, it is our highest expression of care. If you're inspired by the countless citizens nationwide taking part in protecting our democracy, this is your opportunity to show them the profound love in home-cooked food. Most importantly, you don't need to spend lots of money or have lots of skill to do it. Before we begin, these recipes should come with a qualifier: they're simple to make. Here's a list of other considerations when feeding the resistance:

ACCESSIBILITY: Ingredients should be readily available nationwide, even in underserved areas.

SIMPLICITY: The opposite of intimidating. "Skills" should not prevent one from expressing love through cooking. For this, love is the only requirement.

DECOLONIZED/GLOBAL: Though some of the techniques are European, using ingredients that are indigenous to diets around the world will reflect the diversity of those communities you feed.

83

EFFICIENT: Reducing the number of ingredients reduces waste and saves time. Speaking of time, you'll need to give yourself a couple hours to prep this food, but each of the recipes builds on the other.

VEGAN: Though some of these recipes call for butter, if omitted they're still delicious.

Baked Japanese Sweet Potatoes

Like corn, the sweet potato is one of the earliest staple foods of humans. There are few things simpler or more gratifying than a perfectly roasted sweet potato. Mobile roasters serve this simple indulgence, yaki-imo, on the streets of Japan. They are oblong and purple-skinned with yellow flesh, and can be easily split between two people. Most farmers' markets offer them year-round for very little money, three bucks a pound or so. You can use any variety of sweet potato or yam in this recipe. It is one of the most nutritious things we can feed our resisters.

SERVES 8

4 large sweet potatoes (approximately uniform in size)
3 Tbsp olive oil
Sea salt (preferably coarse) or kosher salt

HONEY BUTTER
½ cup [115 g] butter, at room temperature (optional)
Coarse sea salt
1 tsp honey (optional)

Preheat the oven to 400°F [200°C]. Set the rack in the top third of the oven.

Using a fork, stab the potatoes all over so the steam has somewhere to go during baking. (Watch those hands; don't get carried away!) Put the potatoes and olive oil in a large bowl. Using your hands, coat the sweet potatoes in the oil and sprinkle them with a little salt.

Place the sweet potatoes directly on the top rack in the oven. Put a sheet pan on a rack below to catch the dripping oil and any juices released by the potatoes as they bake. Bake until the potatoes are crispy on the outside but give to the pressure of a fork, about 30 minutes. You should be able to seamlessly split it down the center, and should also notice some separation from the skin. If the exterior darkens too quickly, decrease the oven temperature to 350°F [175°C].

If making the honey butter, clean and use the same bowl. Add the butter, lightly sprinkle with coarse sea salt, and add the honey. Whisk vigorously until the butter is light and whipped. Set aside in the fridge.

When the sweet potatoes are ready and still hot, split the potatoes down the center, drop in some honey butter, and enjoy.

Oven-Roasted Tomato Sauce

This tomato sauce is sure be one of the simplest and most reliable tricks in your culinary arsenal. It requires no thought, and tastes exactly the same every time: delicious.

MAKES 3 CUPS [720 ML]

One 28-oz [793-g] can whole peeled tomatoes with
   their juice
4 basil leaves, torn
3 or 4 garlic cloves
1 tsp salt

In a large baking pan, combine the tomatoes with their juice, basil, garlic, and salt. Cover and bake until nearly all of the liquid has evaporated, about 45 minutes. If there's room, you can add the pan to the oven along with the sweet potatoes. When finished, the tomatoes will be more dense, and the garlic soft. Using the tip of the whisk, carefully puncture the tomatoes and lightly crush the sauce. (Unless it's an apron, wearing white is not encouraged.) The resulting texture is that of a rustic, crushed tomato sauce.

Baked Polenta

Polenta, stone-ground corn, is the bread of Northern Italy. Southerners call it grits. Polenta and grits are similar, differing mostly in color and size of the cut of the grain. Their high yield and low cost make them a perfect choice for a crowd. A bag of ground cornmeal should cost only a few dollars at a supermarket; even if you buy the best quality you can afford, those extra few dollars go a very long way.

SERVES 8

1 Tbsp unsalted butter or olive oil, for greasing your pan
2 cups [280 g] cornmeal or polenta (not instant)
3 cups [720 ml] water
1 tsp salt
Unsalted butter (optional)
Freshly ground black pepper

Grease a large, rimmed sheet pan with the butter or olive oil. In a large saucepan, combine the polenta, water, and salt. Increase the heat to high. Grab a glass of wine and a whisk. Your next 10 minutes will be spent alternately drinking and stirring.

The polenta you bought almost certainly contains cornstarch. As the mush begins to boil and bubble you will notice a natural thickening. Hot polenta will begin spitting upward. Careful! Decrease the heat to medium and let the polenta simmer, using the whisk to break up lumps while stirring continuously. If desired, add a generous pat of butter and several grinds of black pepper.

Pour the mixture into the prepared pan. Bake for 30 minutes. The polenta will be perfectly delicious well before then, but it's particularly nice when a crust forms on top.

Now, go clean the polenta pot (it is increasingly difficult to clean as it hardens)!

Depending on the size of your oven, you should be able to finish the sweet potatoes, tomato sauce, and polenta around the same time or at least in succession. The beautiful part about them is that they are perfect to reheat and hard to overcook.

Sweet Potato Cakes (should you make more sweet potatoes than your resisters can finish): Line a sheet pan with parchment paper. Scoop the flesh from the skins of 4 baked sweet potatoes into a saucepan. Add ½ cup [120 ml] of milk or water and 2 lightly beaten eggs. Whisk to combine, cover the pot, and cook over medium heat until the liquid has evaporated, 3 to 5 minutes.

If you have it, grab a ring mold the size of a pint glass rim, and shape round cakes on the prepared sheet pan (or just form the sweet potato mixture into small patties), filling the mold ½ in [12 mm]. Drizzle with olive oil and bake at 350°F [180°C] until the tops are brown and crusty, about 30 minutes. These are delicious warm or reheated in a sauté pan with butter the next morning.

Easy Posole

I have been the chef at Crook's Corner for twenty-four years. Probably, the principal reason I have made it this long is my staff. At least half of them have been with me for fifteen years or more and I love them all. Although I never set out to have this happen, a good portion of them over the years have been immigrants. That's how restaurant kitchens are. Getting to know my staff has been a privilege. In Chapel Hill, we welcome strangers rather than seeing them as threatening. They are just one more thread in the fabric of our community. I learned this recipe from Antonio Lopez, who worked for me for about ten years when I first came to Crook's. He comes from the town of Celaya, Guanajuato in north-central Mexico. He used to make this for staff lunch. One day I had a "duh" moment and put it on the menu. Antonio was eligible for legal status by virtue of the Reagan amnesty, and I am the proud sponsor of him and his family with the INS.

SERVES 6

Kosher salt
One 3-lb [1.3-kg] chicken
2 large carrots, peeled and sliced into thin rounds
6 large tomatillos, quartered

1 fresh jalapeño chile (or more as needed), thinly sliced
  (seeded if you'd like)
1 generous Tbsp dried oregano
One 25-oz [705-g] can Mexican-style hominy, drained
Salt and freshly ground black pepper

Place 8 qt [7.5 L] water and 1 Tbsp kosher salt in a pot large
enough for your chicken to float in. Set the pot over high
heat and bring it to a boil. Add the chicken and let it come
to a boil again. Once it starts boiling again, boil the chicken
until it's just barely cooked through (the meat should be
just opaque throughout), 30 minutes. Turn off the heat
and let the chicken rest in the broth for 15 minutes (it will
continue cooking in the residual heat). Transfer the chicken
to a sheet pan and let it cool. While it's resting, decrease
the heat to low and let the broth simmer away and reduce
a bit as it goes. Once the chicken is cool enough to handle,
pick off the meat from the bones, shred it, and reserve in
a bowl. Return the skin and bones to the pot and let them
simmer in the broth for 20 minutes to infuse their flavor.

Strain the broth into a clean pot (or use a slotted spoon or
a spider to remove and discard the skin and bones). Set it
over medium heat and add the carrots, tomatillos, jalapeño
slices, oregano, and hominy. Cook, stirring now and then,
until the tomatillos collapse and thicken the soup and give
it a citrusy tang, about 15 minutes. Add the shredded
chicken to the soup and let it simmer for a final 10 minutes.

Season the soup to taste with salt and pepper and serve
immediately.

HOW FOOD CAN HELP END RECIDIVISM

By Jordyn Lexton, Executive Director, Drive Change

DISCLAIMER: As long as there are prisons, nothing can end recidivism in America. Our country is fueled by capitalism and capitalism in America is founded on white supremacy. Slavery, Jim Crow, Mass Incarceration—this is the American progression of oppressor and oppression determined by race and inflamed by capitalism. The economic dependency of white men on black and brown bodies runs deep in our history and today. If we're going to end recidivism, we have to think about a new system of justice, one that supports human healing and redistributes power to communities of color via social-conscious consumerism and worker-owned business.

If we are thinking about a new justice system that addresses trauma, food can (and should) play a central role.

FOOD CAN HELP US HEAL.

Cooking and eating are restorative practices for both the chef and the diner; the creative process of cooking is often therapeutic: there is routine, there is aroma, there is taste, there is ownership—the senses are involved and for many, including myself, the act of preparing a meal for someone has healing properties. This can be particularly important for someone who has experienced the trauma of incarceration. The process itself is healing, but so is the outcome: creating something delicious and beautiful for other people can feel extremely rewarding, especially for an individual who may feel that they have had a damaging impact on others and/or society in the past.

The act of eating is also restorative; it is physical and flavorful. Eating is nourishment in action.

Eating someone else's food requires an inherent trust because we are physically taking something someone else prepared and ingesting it into our bodies; that is pretty intimate. Restorative justice is fundamentally about restoring trust.

Genuine human connection is often forged between the person preparing the food and the person consuming it. Food doesn't just connect us to others, it morphs us with others so we become of the same stock. The process of eating is a welcoming of the other into our own bodies. It is the definition of shared humanity. Shared humanity is the lifeline for true justice.

JUSTUS Collard Greens

Begin with the intentions to love and nourish. As you collect your ingredients and prepare the food, think of all the ways your pot of greens will celebrate and support your family and your community. Each time we spend time at the hearth, we have the opportunity to transform our relationship to place and people. When I watched my Grandma make greens, the steam from the pot rising up into her face as she tasted for doneness, she taught me that lesson.

Make your way to your own garden or a neighbor's garden or a community garden and harvest a handful of collard greens. Then visit the farmers' market, go to the stand of your favorite farmer, and purchase three bunches of their freshly picked collard greens. Take time in the garden and at the farmers' market to share your story of collards or other seasonal produce and experiences. All of this talking and learning and caring will make its way into the pot with your collard greens.

SERVES 4 TO 6 SOULS

4 bunches of collard greens (feel free to add beet or turnip tops, kale, or mustard greens if you like)
2 Tbsp olive oil
1 medium yellow onion, chopped
Kosher salt

3 garlic cloves, chopped
3 carrots, chopped
2 cups [480 ml] vegetable broth
Freshly ground black pepper
3 Tbsp apple cider vinegar

As my Aunty says, "clean them greens to your own satis-faction" by removing the large stems and washing them in a bath of salt water or vinegar water. Stack 4 to 6 greens on top of one another, roll together, and slice into ½-in [12-mm] ribbons. Set aside.

Set a deep cast-iron pot over medium-high heat. Once it's hot, add the olive oil, and then add the chopped yellow onion to the pot. Salt slightly to help the onions release their moisture. Decrease the heat to medium and sauté until translucent, stirring occasionally. Add the garlic to the onions and cook over medium heat for an additional 3 minutes, stirring occasionally. Add the carrots and the sliced greens to the pot and pour the vegetable broth over the greens. Season with salt and pepper. Don't stir. Place a tight-fitting lid over the pot, decrease the heat to low, and let the greens steam for 20 minutes. Lift the lid and stir. Add additional broth if your potlikker is low. Replace the lid and cook for an additional 20 minutes. Lift the lid, add the apple cider vinegar, season with salt to taste, and stir again. Replace the lid and cook for another 15 minutes, or until delicious and tender greens show up.

When my big family gathered around to eat Grandma's delicious pot of greens that tasted so much like home, we always sang a blessing first. A song of gratitude. Go ahead and serve the collard greens right from the pot. Serve them with the blessing that all who are nourished by this offering will have even more strength to love and cultivate their community. And don't forget to drink down a jigger full of that potlikker, too.

The People's Grits

In 1969, the Black Panther Party for Self-Defense began
their Free Breakfast for School Children Program out of
St. Augustine's Church in Oakland, California, a program
to insure the survival and self-determination of young black
children. This was a program that J. Edgar Hoover called
"the most dangerous domestic threat to national security."

The goal of the People's Kitchen Collective is not
only to fill our stomachs, but also nourish our souls, feed
our minds, and fuel a movement. We believe food is where
we meet, where we build, where we struggle, and where we
survive. Nearly fifty years later, People's Kitchen Collective
has taken up this powerful legacy of the BPP and cooks
a Free Breakfast each year at the Life Is Living festival in
West Oakland. We serve hundreds of community members
a breakfast made from donations by local food businesses
and urban farms. The menu is often composed of creamy
grits, collard greens, tofu or egg scramble, and sweet
potato biscuits. It is a meal made with love, by community
for community, so that all of us can survive together in the
face of rampant white supremacy and gentrification. This
meal feeds hope and resistance.

SERVES 100 (IN 1-CUP [240-ML] SERVINGS)

25 cups [3.5 kg] grits
12½ qt [12 L] water
6¼ qt [6 L] coconut milk
¼ cup [40 g] kosher salt
1 cup [240 ml] coconut oil

Put the grits in a large, heavy-bottomed stockpot. Add the water. Stir until the water is incorporated, then let the grits settle back to the bottom of the pot. Skim off any debris that was unsettled from the grits. Cover the pot and let the grits soak at room temperature overnight.

The next morning, drain the grits, put the stockpot on the stove, and add the coconut milk and the salt. Over medium heat, proceed to stir and stir the pot until the grits come to a first boil. Decrease the heat to low and let the grits simmer while continuing to stir constantly to prevent burning. Because this is a high volume of grain and liquid the cooking time will be much longer than a traditional grits recipe. Expect to stir the grits for 45 minutes or more.

When the grits are nearly done, add the coconut oil and continue to stir until tender. The grits should be thick enough to coat the back of a spoon. Additional liquid may be needed to reach the desired consistency, so keep a medium pot of hot water going on a side burner and ladle in ½ cup [120 ml] at a time. Wait until each addition of hot water is absorbed before adding another.

Serve the creamy coconut grits hot and full of power to the people!

Tikka Masala Macaroni + Cheese

This macaroni and cheese is on the "Comforting" menu at my restaurant, where we give a dollar from every bowl to a particular non-profit organization. This one specifically supports Destiny Arts Center. We have worked with them for the past four years to support their amazing efforts. They are an incredibly powerful organization that teaches both self-defense and dance to young people on a sliding-fee scale. And more than that, it is a place where young people can express themselves creatively and explore the many issues they may dealing with in their lives, such as racism, sexism, physical abuse, homelessness, drugs, or gangs. In the more than twenty-five years they have been around, the high school graduation rate among kids that are fully integrated in the program is 100 percent. We love them.

SERVES 8

8 green cardamom pods
2 black cardamom pods
One 3-in [7.5-cm] piece cinnamon stick
8 whole cloves
1½ tsp fenugreek seeds
1 Tbsp Indian red chile powder
4 Tbsp [56 g] unsalted butter
1 Tbsp minced peeled fresh ginger

6 garlic cloves, minced
One 6-oz [170-g] can tomato paste
2 cups [480 ml] heavy cream
1 cup [227 g] sour cream
1½ cups [170 g] coarsely grated Cheddar cheese
1½ cups [170 g] coarsely grated Gouda cheese
Kosher salt
1 lb [453 g] elbow macaroni

Place the green and black cardamom pods, cinnamon stick, cloves, and fenugreek seeds in a small skillet set over medium heat. Cook, stirring the spices, until fragrant, about 1 minute. Transfer the toasted spices to a clean coffee grinder and pulse until finely ground (or use a mortar and pestle). Stir in the chile powder and set the mixture aside.

Place the butter in a medium saucepan over medium heat. Once it melts, add the ginger and garlic and cook until sizzling and fragrant, about 1 minute. Add the reserved spice mixture, tomato paste, cream, and ½ cup [120 ml] of water. Whisk everything together until the tomato paste dissolves. Let the mixture heat up until bubbles form around the edge, about 5 minutes, and then whisk in the sour cream and both of the cheeses. Cook, stirring now and then, until the cheeses melt and the sauce is smooth, about 3 minutes. Season the sauce to taste with 2 tsp salt, decrease the heat to low, and keep the sauce warm.

Meanwhile, bring a large pot of water to a boil and season it generously with salt. Add the macaroni and cook according to the package directions. Drain the pasta and return it the pot. Add the cheese sauce and stir well to combine. Serve immediately.

NOTE FROM JULIA: When pressed for time, I have substituted 1 Tbsp of garam masala and 1 Tbsp of regular supermarket red chile powder for Preeti's masala and have had excellent results (not quite as good as real deal toasted and freshly ground spices, but at least it's something homemade).

Red Lentil Soup with Coconut + Cilantro

This soup is the easiest (and fastest!) thing ever and so incredibly satisfying, not to mention a very affordable way to serve a crowd. It's completely vegan, but you could poach a few eggs directly in it before serving if you're looking for some extra protein while still being vegetarian (and/or serve topped with yogurt). Serve in big mugs or in deep bowls filled with rice if you're looking for something even more substantial.

SERVES 8 TO 10

2 Tbsp olive oil

2 large red onions, finely diced

6 garlic cloves, minced

3 Tbsp minced peeled fresh ginger

Kosher salt

One 6-oz [170-g] can tomato paste

2 Tbsp Madras curry powder

2 Tbsp red chile powder

One 13.5-oz [398-g] can coconut milk
  (full-fat or low-fat, up to you)

8 cups [1.4 L] water

2 cups [390 g] red lentils

Finely chopped fresh cilantro leaves and lime wedges
  for serving

Place the olive oil in a large pot set over medium-high heat. Add the onions, garlic, and ginger and sprinkle with a large pinch of salt. Cook, stirring now and then, until the vegetables are softened and starting to brown around the edges, about 12 minutes. Add the tomato paste, curry powder, and chile powder and cook, stirring, until very fragrant, about 1 minute. Whisk in the coconut milk and water and then stir in the lentils along with 1 Tbsp of salt. Increase the heat to high and bring the mixture to a boil. Decrease the heat to low, partially cover the pot, and simmer until the lentils are softened, about 18 minutes (uncover the pot and stir now and then while it's simmering). Season the soup to taste with salt and ladle into bowls.

Top each serving with some cilantro and serve with lime wedges for squeezing over.

Pizza Frittata for a Crowd

With all of the familiar flavors of pizza (roasted tomatoes, basil, and cheese), this frittata gets made on a sheet pan. This means you get a nice, large frittata that cooks evenly and quickly and is very easy to slice and serve. A great, inexpensive option for a group of people getting together in the morning, this frittata also doubles as a vegetarian sandwich filling for meals on the go.

SERVES 8 TO 10

1 lb [453 g] cherry tomatoes
3 garlic cloves, minced
4 Tbsp [60 ml] olive oil, divided
Kosher salt
16 large eggs
Large handful minced fresh basil leaves
8 oz [227 g] firm mozzarella cheese (the one that comes in a block), coarsely grated
1 small handful finely grated Parmesan cheese

Preheat the oven to 425°F [220°C]. Line a sheet pan with parchment paper.

Place the tomatoes and garlic on the prepared sheet pan, drizzle with 3 Tbsp of the olive oil and sprinkle with a large pinch of salt. Use your hands to toss everything together.

Roast the tomatoes, stirring occasionally, until they burst and are tender and concentrated, about 20 minutes.

Meanwhile, place the eggs and basil in a large bowl with 1 tsp of salt. Whisk well to combine.

Using a pastry brush or a folded-up paper towel, wipe the interior edges of the pan with the remaining Tbsp of olive oil. Your future self will thank you when you're not stuck at the sink for longer than you need to be. Make sure the tomatoes are in a nice even layer and then pour the beaten eggs over them. Evenly sprinkle the mozzarella and Parmesan on top of the eggs.

Return the sheet pan to the oven and bake until the eggs are just set and a little bit puffed, about 15 minutes. Let the frittata cool for at least 10 minutes before cutting into squares for serving. It's equally good at room temperature.

Go-To Muhammara Dip

This completely vegan, completely easy-to-make dip is the perfect thing to take to your book-club-turned-political-resistance group. It takes no time to prepare, but tastes like it did. Serve as a dip for warm pita bread or pita chips, raw vegetables, or crackers.

MAKES ABOUT 2 CUPS [480 ML]

One 12-oz [340-g] jar roasted red peppers, drained
¾ cup [100 g] walnuts, lightly toasted
2 small garlic cloves, minced
2 Tbsp olive oil
2 tsp pomegranate molasses (or fresh lemon juice),
   plus more as needed
½ tsp kosher salt, plus more as needed
½ tsp ground cumin
½ tsp ground cayenne pepper

Place all the ingredients in the bowl of a food processor fitted with the metal blade and pulse until thoroughly combined and spreadable but not completely smooth (this is nice with a little bit of texture). Season to taste with salt and/or pomegranate molasses (or lemon juice) as needed. Serve immediately.

Leftovers can be stored in a covered container in the refrigerator for up to a week, but bring to room temperature and season to taste before serving.

BAKED GOODS +

PORTABLE
SNACKS

Persistence Biscuits

Hot buttered soul food and a basket full of biscuits bring people to my Sunday Supper dinners in Atlanta. Seated around the table, they find common ground and fried chicken, fostering relationships that help us work better together as a community. As the menu changes with each dinner, these biscuits remain by request, along with a few extra you can take home with you. These are little rounds of baked dough that are made with the same biscuit recipe I watched my grandmother make on Sundays and serve to the kids she felt might not have money for breakfast. Now the biscuits help fund programs that teach computer science to kids in under-represented communities in Atlanta. Let the flaky layers of these biscuits warm your soul and grace your table. Invite some folks over to break bread with and make an impact in the lives of those around you. If you're feeding a crowd, bake smaller biscuits or make several batches of this recipe.

MAKES 1 DOZEN

3 cups [360 g] all-purpose flour, plus more for your
   work surface
1 Tbsp baking powder
½ tsp baking soda
1 tsp salt

2 Tbsp solid vegetable shortening, chilled and cut into ½-in [12-mm] chunks

8 Tbsp [1 stick/112 g] unsalted butter, chilled and thinly sliced, plus 2 melted Tbsp

1¾ cups [420 ml] chilled buttermilk

1 tsp cane syrup

Adjust the oven rack to the middle position and preheat to 450°F [230°C].

In a large bowl, whisk together the flour, baking powder, baking soda, and salt. Work the shortening into the flour mix by breaking the shortening into chunks with your fingertips until only pea-size pieces remain. Work in the butter slices the same way until all of the butter is incorporated. Freeze the mixture for 15 minutes.

Add the buttermilk to the chilled flour mixture, stirring with a fork until the dough forms into a ball and no dry bits of flour are visible (the dough will be soft, shaggy, and sticky). Turn the dough out onto a floured surface and dust lightly with more flour. With floured hands, pat the dough into a rectangle about ¼ in [6 mm] thick. Fold the dough into thirds, dusting lightly with flour as needed (don't be shy, it might need quite a bit as you shape it since the dough is so soft). Pat into a rectangle again. Lift the short end of the folded dough and fold into thirds again, forming a rectangle. Repeat this process, folding and patting the dough into rectangles that are ½ in [12 mm] thick, 2 more times for a total of 3 rounds of folding. Cut the dough into 12 rounds using a 2-in [5-cm] biscuit cutter. Be sure to firmly press the cutter straight down into the dough. Do not twist the cutter, as twisting will seal off the biscuit edges, preventing the biscuits from rising.

Evenly space the biscuits on an ungreased baking sheet. (**A NOTE FROM JT**: bake the scraps too and enjoy them as a snack!) Place the 2 Tbsp of melted butter in a small bowl with the cane syrup and whisk together. Brush the tops of the biscuits with the mixture.

Bake until golden brown, about 15 minutes. Remove the biscuits from the oven and allow to cool slightly before serving.

FROM JT

Baked Oatmeal + Apple Squares

These baked oatmeal bars are the easiest way to make oatmeal not only portable, but also really packed with flavor
and long-lasting energy from things such as grated apple
and ground flaxseed. They're great whether you're headed
to a march or just driving your kid to school and need
something healthy to eat on-the-go. If you don't have or
like apple, you can use two handfuls of fresh or frozen blue-
berries or raspberries (no need to thaw if frozen), or even
grated sweet potato or carrot. These can also be served for
dessert if you warm them up and top them with ice cream.

MAKES NINE 2½-IN [6-CM] SQUARES

Baking spray
2 large eggs, beaten
2 Tbsp honey
1 cup [240 ml] whole milk
2 tsp vanilla extract
1 tsp baking powder
1 tsp kosher salt
2 tsp ground cinnamon
3 Tbsp ground flaxseed
2 cups [170 g] old-fashioned rolled oats
1 large apple (any kind), peeled, seeded,
    and coarsely grated

Preheat the oven to 350°F [175°C]. Spray an 8-in [20-cm] square baking pan with nonstick baking spray. Line the bottom with parchment paper and spray that too just to be safe.

Place the eggs and honey in a large bowl and whisk well to combine. Add the milk and vanilla and give it another whisk. Sprinkle the baking powder, salt, and cinnamon on top and whisk well to combine. Add the ground flaxseed, oats, and apple and stir well to combine everything. Transfer the mixture to the prepared baking pan. Spread it out so that it's in an even layer and press it down with a rubber spatula.

Bake until the oatmeal is firm to the touch and golden brown on top, about 35 minutes. Let the oatmeal cool for at least 15 minutes and then transfer it to a cutting board. Cut it into nine 2½-in [6-cm] squares.

Serve warm or at room temperature.

Leftovers can be stored in an airtight container in the refrigerator for up to 3 days or wrapped well and frozen for up to 3 months (defrost and warm in a toaster oven or 300°F [150°C] oven before eating).

Coconut + Almond Granola

This simple, incredibly crunchy granola is great for break-fast with berries and yogurt or any type of milk, or it can be enjoyed straight out of the jar for a quick snack. It also makes for a great ice cream topping. The lightly whipped egg whites help you forego lots of fat and sugar, but feel free to omit them if you're vegan and add an extra Tbsp of olive oil (and substitute maple syrup for the honey). One quick tip: measure the oil before the honey so that the honey can slip out of your measuring cup very easily.

MAKES ABOUT 5 CUPS [500 G]

2 large egg whites
¼ cup [60 ml] olive oil
¼ cup [60 ml] honey
2 tsp kosher salt
1 tsp ground cinnamon
2½ cups [213 g] old-fashioned rolled oats
1 cup [75 g] unsweetened coconut flakes
1 cup [90 g] sliced almonds

Preheat the oven to 350°F [175°C]. Line a sheet pan with parchment paper and set it aside.

Place the egg whites in a large bowl and whisk until they begin to foam and are opaque, almost like a wave crashing. Add the olive oil, honey, salt, and cinnamon and whisk well to combine. Add the oats, coconut flakes, and almonds and stir well to combine.

Transfer the mixture to the prepared sheet pan and spread it out so that it's in an even layer. Bake the granola, stirring it every 10 minutes, until it's dark golden brown, about 25 minutes total.

Let the granola cool completely before transferring it to a glass jar (a plastic container will encourage it to get soggy). It will crisp as it cools. Store it covered in a dark spot for up to a week.

Sweet Potato Tzimmes Muffins

These healthy muffins taste so much like tzimmes, the mixture of stewed root vegetables and dried fruit traditionally served during Passover. Made with 100 percent whole-wheat flour, lots of grated sweet potatoes, buttermilk, and olive oil, these are truly good for you. There are some chopped prunes (which could be raisins or any dried fruit), plus a bit of honey, and lots of warm spices to add sweetness. Serve with coffee or tea in the morning or the afternoon, or try serving them alongside Red Lentil Soup with Coconut + Cilantro (page 101). These are also wonderfully portable and a great option for marches, meetings, and bake sales.

MAKES 12 MUFFINS

1½ cups [180 g] whole-wheat flour
1½ tsp baking powder
½ tsp baking soda
1 tsp kosher salt
2 tsp ground cinnamon
2 tsp ground ginger
½ tsp ground cloves
2 large eggs, lightly beaten
¾ cup [180 ml] buttermilk
¼ cup [60 ml] olive oil
¼ cup [60 ml] honey
1 Tbsp vanilla extract

2 cups [280 g] peeled and coarsely grated sweet potatoes
  (about 1 medium sweet potato)
½ cup [70 g] diced prunes or raisins

Preheat the oven to 375°F [190°C]. Line a standard
12-cup muffin tin with paper liners.

Place the whole-wheat flour, baking powder, baking soda,
salt, cinnamon, ginger, and cloves in a large bowl and whisk
together.

Place the eggs, buttermilk, olive oil, honey, and vanilla in
another large bowl and whisk them together. Using a rubber spatula, stir the flour mixture into the egg mixture and
then gently fold in the grated sweet potatoes and prunes.

Divide the batter among the lined muffin cups (the batter
will fill the cups).

Bake the muffins until dark brown, firm to the touch,
incredibly fragrant, and a toothpick inserted into the center of a muffin comes out clean, 35 to 40 minutes. Let the
muffins cool in the tin set on a wire cooling rack for at least
15 minutes before eating.

Serve warm or at room temperature.

Spiced Brown Sugar Pound Cake with Rum Molasses Glaze

A pound cake nourishes your soul like none other. It is the type of therapy that restores you and prepares you for the battles of the resistance. In my family, we make pound cakes for celebrations and life's most unsettling times. It is our way of coping and evoking comfort when our spirits most need it. This cake has so much warmth and sass, calm and intensity. The molasses glaze perfectly complements the hint of molasses in the brown sugar cake batter, and my favorite part is when those notes of rum awaken your palette. When your soul needs food in the midst of the fight, this is the cake to make.

SERVES 10

Nonstick baking spray (such as Baker's Joy)
1½ cups [340 g] unsalted butter, at room temperature
2 cups [400 g] packed light brown sugar
¾ cup [150 g] granulated sugar
1 tsp kosher salt
5 large eggs, at room temperature
3 cups [360 g] sifted all-purpose flour
1 cup [120 g]sour cream, at room temperature
1 Tbsp plus 1 tsp vanilla extract

1½ tsp ground cinnamon
1 tsp ground nutmeg
½ tsp ground ginger
¼ tsp ground cloves
1 cup [120 g] confectioners' sugar
1 Tbsp molasses
2 Tbsp rum

Preheat the oven to 325°F [160°C]. Spray a 10-cup [2.3 L] Bundt pan with nonstick baking spray.

Place the butter, brown sugar, granulated sugar, and salt in the bowl of a stand mixer fitted with the whisk attachment and mix on high speed until light and fluffy, 5 minutes. Add the eggs, one at a time, and mix until well incorporated. Slow the mixer to its lowest speed and carefully add in the flour in intervals of 1 cup [120 g]. Add the sour cream and the 1 Tbsp of vanilla. Mix in the cinnamon, nutmeg, ginger, and cloves until just combined.

Pour the batter into the prepared pan and bake until a toothpick inserted into the center comes out moist but mostly clean, 65 to 75 minutes.

Cool the cake for 10 minutes then invert onto a cooling rack and cool to room temperature.

In a small bowl, whisk together the confectioners' sugar, molasses, rum, and the remaining 1 tsp of vanilla until smooth and pourable. Drizzle over the cake and serve.

Chocolate Espresso Pie Bars

During the 1950s, a group of women baked and sold pies, cookies, and cakes in beauty salons and on street corners to help fund transportation costs during the bus boycott triggered by Rosa Parks in Montgomery, Alabama. Georgia Gilmore's secret kitchen known as "The Club From Nowhere" used her cooking talent to fund and feed the Civil Rights Movement. These decadent pie bars will get you fueled up and ready to go!

MAKES FORTY-EIGHT 2-IN [5-CM] BARS

CRUST
4½ cups [540 g] unbleached all-purpose flour
¾ cup [150 g] packed light brown sugar
¾ tsp fine sea salt
1 lb [4 sticks/448 g] unsalted butter, melted, plus a little extra for your pan

FILLING
1 cup [165 g] chocolate chips (we used 70 percent cacao)
1½ cups [3 sticks/339 g] unsalted butter, cut into large cubes
1 Tbsp vanilla extract
3 cups [600 g] sugar
1 Tbsp ground espresso

1 tsp ground cinnamon
½ tsp salt
6 large eggs

Confectioners' sugar for dusting
Ice cream (any flavor you like such as vanilla or coffee,
    for serving [optional])

To make the crust, position a rack in the middle of the oven
and preheat the oven to 350°F [180°C]. Lightly butter the
bottom and sides of a 12-by-17-in [30-by-43-cm] rimmed
baking sheet, then line with parchment paper. Allow the
ends to hang over on all sides to help lift the bars from
the pan.

In a large bowl, use your hands to combine the flour, brown
sugar, and salt (break up any large clumps of brown sugar
with your fingers). Slowly drizzle in the butter and stir with
a fork until the mixture looks moist and crumbly. Using
your hands, press the dough evenly over the bottom and up
the sides of the baking sheet. You can decorate the edges
by crimping with a fork or leave them rustic. Chill in the
refrigerator until firm, about 15 minutes.

Line the pie shell with parchment and fill with dried beans.
Bake until the crust is just set and lightly browned, 12 to
15 minutes. Remove the beans and set the crust aside on a
wire rack to cool to room temperature.

To make the filling, decrease the temperature to 325°F [165°C]. In a heat-proof bowl set over a saucepan of simmering water, melt the chocolate chips with the butter over medium heat, stirring occasionally, until smooth, about 5 minutes. Stir in the vanilla. Remove from the heat and whisk in the sugar, espresso, cinnamon, and salt. Mix until incorporated. Whisk in the eggs, one at a time. Pour the filling into the cooled crust. Bake until set in the center and cracks form on the top, 45 to 50 minutes.

Now the hard part: set aside to cool completely. When cool, cut into forty-eight roughly 2-by-2-in [5-by-5-cm] bars. Dust the tops with confetioners' sugar and you're ready to go.

Serve with ice cream, if you like.

Angel Food Bread Pudding with Butterscotch Sauce

Every Thursday morning my wife, Grace, and I wake up before the sun comes out and drive half an hour to a church we are not members of. We roll up our sleeves in the church's kitchen with four other people, including Georgine, our ninety-year-old friend, to cook a meal for sixty people in our community who are homebound for a variety of reasons including chronic illness. We package up the meals and a group of volunteers delivers them. I have never been a morning person, but I've come to look forward to Thursday mornings more than any other day of the week. I love this group of people and the food we make, and it means so much to have a tangible way to give back to our community. Here is my bread pudding recipe that I make there often (it's the best way to stretch a ton of leftover bread into something really delicious). If you're baking for sixty as I normally do, feel free to triple this. If you skip the Butterscotch Sauce, increase the sugar to 1 full cup [200 g] to compensate (but I highly recommend making the sauce).

SERVES 20

Baking spray

1 lb [453 g] white or whole-wheat sandwich bread,
   torn or cut into bite-size pieces

1 lb [453 g] cinnamon-raisin sandwich bread,
   torn or cut into bite-size pieces

One 14-oz [397-g] can sweetened condensed milk

½ cup [100 g] granulated sugar

4 cups [1 L] whole milk

1½ Tbsp vanilla extract

2 tsp kosher salt

1 Tbsp ground cinnamon

1 cup [240 ml] heavy cream

12 large eggs

Butterscotch Sauce (page 125)

Preheat the oven to 400°F [200°C]. Spray the bottoms
and sides of a 12-by-18-in [30-by-46-cm] roasting pan
(basically whatever you would roast a turkey in and a dis-
posable aluminum pan is totally fine) with baking spray.

Place all of the bread in the roasting pan.

Place the sweetened condensed milk, sugar, milk, vanilla,
and salt in a large pot set over high heat. Warm the mixture, stirring now and then to dissolve the sugar, until
bubbles form at the edge and then turn off the heat.

Place the cinnamon in a very large bowl with half the cream and whisk well to form a paste. Add the rest of the cream and whisk well to dissolve the paste and then crack all of the eggs into the bowl and whisk well to combine (making the cinnamon paste helps it incorporate evenly). Ladle in about 1 cup [240 ml] of the hot milk mixture and whisk well to combine. Repeat the process a few more times to gently warm up the eggs. Add whatever remains of the hot milk mixture to the eggs and whisk well. Pour the custard over the bread and stir well to combine (I use my hands to do this). Press the bread pieces down to make sure they're all submerged in the custard.

Bake the bread pudding until golden brown, set throughout (test by jiggling the pan), and slightly puffed, about 40 minutes. Serve warm with the Butterscotch Sauce drizzled on top.

Butterscotch Sauce

MAKES ABOUT 2 CUPS [480 ML]

8 Tbsp [1 stick/112 g] unsalted butter
1 cup [200 g] packed dark brown sugar
1½ cups [360 ml] heavy cream
2 tsp kosher salt
1 Tbsp vanilla extract

Place the butter, brown sugar, cream, and salt in a medium saucepan set over high heat. Once it comes to a boil, decrease the heat and simmer, stirring now and then, until slightly reduced, about 15 minutes. Turn off the heat and stir in the vanilla.

Serve warm. You can also cool it to room temperature, store it in a covered container in the refrigerator for up to a week, and then reheat in a saucepan set over low heat until warm.

TWENTY PLACES TO REACH OUT TO

- Get help if you need it.

- Ask what kind of support they need and offer it if you can.

- Offer specific, tangible things you can do to support whatever they do (this could be money, translation services, rides, meals, childcare, and more).

- Let them know you support what they do and what they stand for.

LOCAL

1. LGBTQ Centers
2. Churches, synagogues, mosques, and other places of worship
3. Public libraries
4. Public schools
5. First responders
6. Food pantries
7. Domestic violence shelters
8. Town board and precinct meetings: go and be in the room where it happens, especially on the local level

STATE AND NATIONAL

9. Capitol Switch Board: 202-224-3121 (call to be directed to your senators and state representatives)

10. Subscribe to and support letters of record and newspapers with integrity

SPECIFIC GROUPS

11. ACLU (American Civil Liberties Union)

12. SURJ (Showing Up for Racial Justice)

13. Black Lives Matter

14. Southern Poverty Law Center

15. Trans Lifeline

16. Planned Parenthood

17. IRAP (International Refugee Assistance Project)

18. UNEP (United Nations Environmental Programme)

19. Greenpeace

20. Girls Inc.

TEN WAYS TO ENGAGE THAT AREN'T SO OBVIOUS

1. Know your power as a consumer and vote with your wallet. Research the stores and companies you normally purchase from. Consider both boycotts and buycotts—in other words, don't spend your money on companies and institutions that don't share your values, and go out of your way to support those that do. Check out resources like grabyourwallet.org for more information.

2. Research the campaign laws in your local areas and take down outdated campaign material in public spaces and inform local officials about outdated campaign materials in private spaces.

3. Make cookies or banana bread or something like that (or buy something like that) and bring to the first responders in your neighborhood or to the folks who work at your public library and thank them for their service.

4. Take a self-defense class and bring someone with you.

5. Become a reliable mentor to someone. Do this through an established organization like Big Brothers Big Sisters or through your work, alma mater,

community, or even family. Be accountable to that person. Help them set goals and support them as they meet those goals. Show up.

6. Sign up to help escort someone to an abortion appointment. Call places that provide them in your area to make yourself available for this.

7. Carve out some time to do what you already do for people who don't have access to your services. For example, if you're an accountant, help teach someone how to budget or prepare their taxes. If you're a graphic designer, contact a local activism group and see if they need a flyer or logo designed. If you teach students finance or business, make a local business your class project and get it off the ground. Do what you already do, but with a little bit more purpose.

8. Teach your children, or those in your life if you do not have children, about something or someone they do not know. Visibility is so valuable. Make sure they are aware that someone who looks like them can achieve anything and give them actual examples.

9. Look into what after-school programs are available in your area. If there aren't enough, help support or create one.

10. Run for office! Or support someone you believe in.

TEN THINGS YOU CAN DO IN LESS THAN TEN MINUTES

1. Make sure you're registered to vote. If you're not, register. If you are, call a friend and make sure that they are and ask them to do the same.

2. Subscribe to a newsletter like Mikki's tinyletter.com /actionnow or 2hoursaweek.org and commit to reading it and following up on their suggested actions. Unsubscribe from any newsletters that do not inspire you to take action.

3. Call your representatives. Tell them (or someone on their staff) why you support what they're doing or tell them why their decision/action does NOT represent you. If it's busy, call again.

4. Call your local school system, whether or not you have a child in it, and ask if they have a gender-neutral bathroom. If they don't, set aside a few minutes a day to keep calling, or better yet show up, until they create one and get neighbors and friends to do the same.

5. Think about small ways to impact the environment and commit to at least one (for example, bring your own reusable cup to the coffee shop or an empty water bottle to the airport and fill it after you go through security and use it for your entire trip).

6. If you're making plans for a meal, choose a restaurant run by someone who doesn't look like you. This might be an immigrant, a person of color, or someone who is LGBTQ. If there is something on the menu you're not familiar with, ask about it.

7. Look up who and what your bank supports and consider whether they're the right ones to hold onto your money.

8. Buy a book by an author who has had a different life experience than you. Read it, for at least 10 minutes a day, and then give it to someone else who will also benefit from reading it.

9. Tell someone about your activism or share it on social media. Make yourself accountable to someone else.

10. Do a random act of kindness without expecting anything in return.

ACKNOWLEDGMENTS

Thank you, thank you, thank you to:

All of the incredible contributors who rallied and responded so quickly and thoughtfully. Thank you for bringing your light into this project.

Kari Stuart, the best champion a writer could ask for, for making this happen. I'm so proud to work with you.

Sarah Billingsley for saying yes. Especially while I was on deadline to write a whole different book for you.

Vanessa Dina for jumping on board and making this look and feel so good.

Alexandra Brown, Amy Cleary, and Albee Dalbotten for getting the word out there and doing it with kindness.

Christine Carswell and Tyrrell Mahoney for being so supportive.

Tera Killip, Steve Kim, and Shona Burns in Production, Sara Waitt in Managing Editorial, and everyone else who wanted or worked on this book.

My friends and family, who constantly teach me so much. And for their buoying support.

My darling Grace, you inspire me not only to dream, but to do. Life is so much bigger, more meaningful, surprising, and full of love with you. Hope, Winky, and Turk, you make home the best place in the world.

CONTRIBUTORS

ALI STONE

Jocelyn Delk Adams
Author of *Grandbaby Cakes* and Founder of Grandbaby-Cakes.com, Chicago, IL

ANNA SODZIAK

Maya-Camille Broussard
Owner, Justice of the Pies, Chicago, IL

CHELSEY LUGER

Anthony Thosh Collins
Co-founder, wellforculture.com, Scottsdale, AZ

ANDREW THOMAS LEE

Erika Council
Blogger at Southern Soufflé and runs the Sunday Supper Club, Atlanta, GA

FRANISE HEARN

Devita Davison
Executive Director, FoodLab Detroit, Detroit, MI

RINNE ALLEN

Cheryl Day
Baker, Author, Back in the Day Bakery, Savannah, GA

ELLA COLLEY

A. R. TANG

SEAN SANTIAGO

Von Diaz
Food Writer and
Radio Producer,
New York, NY

Yana Gilbuena
Culinary Nomad/Chef,
San Francisco, CA

Mikki Halpin
Author of *It's Your
World: If You Don't Like
It, Change It*, Creator of
tinyletter.com/actionnow,
Brooklyn, NY

GEMMA FLEMING

JORDAN ROQUE

LIZ CLAYMAN

Hawa Hassan
CEO Basbaas Sauce,
New York, NY

Callie Jayne
Lead Organizer, Citizen
Action of New York,
Hudson Valley, NY

Jordyn Lexton
Executive Director,
Drive Change,
Brooklyn, NY

THOSH COLLINS

Chelsey Luger
Co-founder,
wellforculture.com,
Scottsdale, AZ

ALANNA HALE

Preeti Mistry
Author, Chef, and
Owner, Juhu Beach
Club and Navi Kitchen,
Oakland, CA

MOLLY DECOUDREAUX

**People's Kitchen
Collective: Sita
Bhaumik, Jocelyn
Jackson, Saqib Keval**
Co-founders of PKC,
Oakland, CA

AUDREY LARROW

Stephen Satterfield
Writer, Speaker, Multi-
media Producer, and
Founder of Whetstone
Magazine, Oakland, CA

NIK SHARMA

Nik Sharma
Food Writer, Cook,
Photographer, and San
Francisco Chronicle
columnist, A Brown
Table, Oakland, CA

SANA JAVERI KADRI

Shakirah Simley
Co-Founder and Orga-
nizer, Nourish|Resist,
San Francisco, CA

SOLEIL KUNKLE

RUBEN HUGHES

MOYO OYELOLA

Bill Smith
Chef, Crook's Corner,
Chapel Hill, NC

Bryant Terry
Author, Chef, and
Chef-in-Residence
at the Museum of
the African Diaspora,
San Francisco, CA

Tunde Wey
Writer, Cook, Founder,
Blackness in America
dinner series,
New Orleans, LA

SARAH PEET

Caleb Zigas
Executive Director
of La Cocina, San
Francisco, CA

We are at our best...
when a salad bowl of hand picked greens are passed...
a lovingly prepared delicious casserole...hand crafted...
garnished herbal beans gathered...seasoned...prepared...
living to feed those in need...working for our liberties...
with care...love unyielding...cooking for peace...my recipe...
stirring our shared cause...sauce...a spoonful at a time for all...
so let there be healthy dining...food that's life sustaining...
as we break bread...together...defending our basic rights...

—ALEXANDER SMALLS,
Executive Chef and Co-owner, Minton's and The Cecil